D1083461

Planning and Education

By the same author

The Education Officer and his World

with Anne Dufton
An Equal Chance

Planning and Education

Derek Birley
Director   The Northern Ireland Polytechnic

Routledge & Kegan Paul
London and Boston

First published 1972
by Routledge & Kegan Paul Ltd
Broadway House, 68–74 Carter Lane
London EC4V 5EL and
9 Park Street,
Boston, Mass. 02108, U.S.A.

Printed in Great Britain
by Richard Clay (The Chaucer Press), Ltd.,
Bungay, Suffolk

ISBN 0 7100 7281 3

Contents

Introduction

This book is intended, primarily, for educationists interested in planning and planners interested in education. It is not, however, meant only for experts or even only for professionals. Its approach is exploratory and its purpose introductory, so it may have something to offer to a much wider range of people.

It is certainly not a book for witch-doctors, or for those who believe in witch-doctors. It does not pretend, that is, to offer magical solutions to profound problems through mastery of special techniques. Of course, in both planning and education there is considerable scope for expertise. Yet they are both, in the end, activities practised by human beings for other human beings, which suggests that we should constantly bear in mind the limits, as well as the scope, of our technical knowledge and skill.

I have always liked the Buddhist story about the blind men who were confronted by an elephant and asked to describe it. One, catching hold of the trunk, thought it was a snake; another felt its ear and declared it was a palm leaf; the one who felt its body thought it a wall; the man by its leg suggested a tree; and the one who held the tail said it was a brush. They soon began quarrelling, each claiming to know the truth.

Our notions of life are inevitably limited, governed by the bits of evidence that happen to come our way. Yet we are curious; we feel the need to identify, to speculate. In fact we often seek to impose patterns of our own devising on things much more complex than we can comprehend. For many of us this is satisfying, and even necessary, but we are wise if we accept that, in such matters, our perception is likely to be distorted. Our interpretations of human affairs may indeed be even more naïve than those of the blind men with their elephant, which, for all its size and peculiar shape, is at least tangible and finite.

The approach to planning suggested here, then, is one that tries to be constantly aware of its own limitations; one that is not merely analytical but self-analytical; one that regularly questions basic assumptions. This has implications not only for methods but also for the language in which they are expressed. For one thing, an esoteric vocabulary can give a misleading impression of certainty. For another, it is more important that the blind men should be able to communicate with each other than that one should seek to impress or baffle the others.

So, at the risk of offending an occasional pundit, the book is written in the plainest language I can muster. The way the education service is managed is too important to us all for it to be discussed in terms impenetrable to the intelligent layman. I shall need to use some jargon at times, but it will be kept to a minimum and explained when it is first used. Above all I hope to avoid using it as mumbo-jumbo, the kind of magic language sometimes offered as an alternative, rather than an aid, to thought.

The underlying problems of planning our education service are profound. How far can the need to evaluate such a costly enterprise be reconciled with its essential freedom? What criteria can we use for the evaluation? How can we reconcile democracy with efficiency? How far are business methods applicable to educational management? How can we plan in our sort of society? How realistic is planning when applied to education?

The book does not profess to offer answers to these mind-bending questions, but suggests rather that in such matters the important thing is that the questions should be asked. The planning process outlined here is one in which the value lies as much in the asking as in any 'results' it may produce. Above all it is one by which planning can become a meaningful exercise in which everyone plays a part, rather than a bag of tricks displayed by a few experts.

This approach, highly desirable in any application of planning, seems especially necessary in the social services. In educational planning, I shall argue, it is not just a requirement of democracy that educators themselves, at all levels, should be involved, but an essential basis of any planning that goes beyond the superficial. Teachers throughout the education service; school, college and university administrators; education officers—their impact on the service should be positive rather than a reaction to external stimuli. They need to see techniques and organisation (and those who provide them) in their proper perspective, as means, not ends in themselves. And to do this they need to participate fully.

The exposition in the second part of the book of the technique known as planning–programming–budgeting has the possibility of participation very much in mind. It does not aim at sophistication nor at presenting tablets from the mountain top. Although in its fullest development the approach represents a total system for the education service as a whole, I have tried here simply to outline the modest beginnings of such an exercise, in the belief that individuals and small groups can apply the method, with profit and perhaps even with pleasure, to a whole range of planning activities, small as well as great.

1 Directions

Man needs his dreams. One of the most persistent is that of a rational order as the informing spirit of our universe. The concepts of peace, social justice, prosperity and enlightenment that have been built on this assumption have varied widely. Sometimes individuals or groups, sitting pretty in their own little corner at their own little moment of time, have suggested that the ideal has already been achieved. More often the sustaining vision has been of mankind moving, either directly or in evolutionary fashion, towards a perfect, or at least a better, world.

Whether these dreams subsequently seem to have been based on precognition—blurred or distorted but recognisable—or the merest illusion appears to make very little difference to us. We have acquired (or been given) an extraordinary talent for rationalisation; an ability to explain in terms of conscious reasoning what may have been unconsciously motivated. Our memories are, fortunately for our sanity, selective, rejecting what we cannot bear to recall. Even if these phenomena have an existence merely in our minds, they are very useful tricks, and we should be thankful for the part they have played in ensuring, so far, the survival of our particular species. If they are something more, a compulsive striving by an evolving individual component of an evolving total system to comprehend the pattern of the whole, then man's unceasing struggle to turn his dream into reality may seem less forlorn.

Comprehending is nowadays generally seen as an essential prelude to controlling those uncertain elements of existence that have been regarded as the main threats to civilisation. In earlier societies magic, with the promise of subduing these elements, and then primitive religion, with the hope of propitiating them, seemed to offer short-cuts. The approach of latter-day institutions has been more circum-spect. The ethical religions, for example, have been concerned with securing less tangible rewards. And science, after an exhilarating flourish or two, has appeared increasingly reluctant to concern itself with predicting the outcome of its discoveries.

Not surprisingly we find conflicting attitudes on what should be the proper relationship between knowledge and social action. Some complain that statesmen are dominated by theoreticians; others that they do not make enough use of available expertise. Conversely, scholars are frequently apprehensive about the possible corruption of their learning by applying it to the political world. And there is growing awareness of the need to involve laymen if the decisions of

1

men of action or the advice of men of knowledge are to be success-fully applied. Nowhere are these dilemmas more acute than in the technique of social action we call planning. The application of expertise to the most fundamental human prob-lems has, in fact, a discouraging history. Nor does our modern habit of narrowing the field of operation always improve matters. The per-formance of magicians and soothsayers was not necessarily less successful in shaping constructive social policy than that of economic advisers today. For one thing, though our ancestors may have been wildly wrong in assuming that certain actions produced certain re-sults, we are rarely in a position to trace our way through the maze of complex interactions in modern life with enough certainty to know what causes precisely what. And the fragmentation of knowledge that comes from the search for greater certainty through specialisa-tion brings with it problems of communication so immense as to have given birth to a whole new science.

Planning and the education service

In applying planning to education there are, of course, special problems. To establish objectives for the education service amid the uncertain values of our profit-oriented brand of democracy is ex-ceptionally difficult; and the process of trying to achieve them has inherent complications. The result exemplifies in an acute form the basic tension between the requirements of planning and of freedom.

When governments or authorities make decisions that affect our lives, we often, whether we agree with them or not, feel vulnerable, like pawns in someone else's game. By now most people accept the basic proposition that if a nation with limited resources is to make the best use of them, and avoid the extremes of social injustice, planning is necessary. Yet the characteristic reaction to particular planning decisions is often to put freedom first. The resulting tension is clearly evident in most of our social institutions, spectacularly so in the education service.

On the one hand, we cannot allow the service to drift along aim-lessly. It is too costly, too important to our future economic pros-perity. On the other hand, it is too crucial for democracy (which depends in the end on the calibre of the voters), too valuable in pre-serving the possibility of reform, too vital for the integrity and the dignity of the individual for us to allow it to be circumscribed by political or bureaucratic considerations or by expediency. So, where-as all planning walks a tightrope, educational planning treads a par-ticularly high, thin strand.

Throughout this book I shall argue that one of the pre-conditions of planning for education is that everyone engaged in the service, professionally or voluntarily, should be involved in its planning. This is not merely because joining the ranks of the planners rather than the planned may reduce the hostility many educators—often as the result of bitter experience—feel towards those who shape their destinies. Nor is it simply that it is a requirement of a democratic education service. Above all, it is because only thus is the tension between the demands of efficiency and of democracy likely to be satisfactorily resolved.

The proposition is not based on the romantic notion that involving more people is in itself likely to improve planning. Without proper attention to techniques great participation can be counter-productive. Without an appropriate organisation plans cannot be implemented. Without improved communication the whole process will be ineffective. What it does imply, however, is that these are in the end secondary questions, and that there is a prior and overriding need to consider fundamentals, to seek out new directions of thought in which planning can be united with what it seeks to plan.

Are there basic similarities, for example, between the processes of planning and of educating? If so, can we develop a philosophy of planning as a natural extension of identified educational needs? Can this philosophy be expressed in a common language, one that seeks to convey, not to conceal information? These are some of the questions to be explored at the outset if techniques are to be any more than superficial tricks, and organisation any more than an interesting aspect of the sociological curriculum.

Planning and organisation

In Britain, education, like the other social services, can point with some satisfaction to steady improvement in techniques over the years. In planning—developing policy and bringing about necessary changes smoothly and economically—the record is much less impressive. Significantly, proposals for educational development seem increasingly to be expressed in terms of organisational change; for example, in such matters as the age of transfer to secondary school, the pattern of secondary education, and the binary system in higher education. Recent reports on the other social services—Seebohm, the 1970 Green Paper on the health services, the Royal Commission on local government—have also been preoccupied with machinery and organisation. These preoccupations coincide with a sharp decline in the strength and coherence of the principles underlying the services.

Of course it is hardly surprising if poor organisation is regarded as the chief enemy of social progress. In education there is plenty of evidence that the pattern of decision-making is diffuse, vague and haphazard. Why, for example, on such a tiny, crowded island do we tolerate diverse interpretations of national policy in the age and methods of transfer to secondary schools? We should rather ask what else could happen even if the government wished to standardise the situation. The interplay of local and national agencies, laymen and professionals, teachers and administrators, researchers and politicians, produces complex patterns of control in which authoritative decision-making has no place. The financial and legislatory constraints of the service are equally complex, with Treasury, Department of Education and Science (DES), local council and education committee each playing a part.

Indeed our education system is just as much a product as a determinant of social forces. So much of the British talent for compromise has gone into its creation that only the tolerant and pragmatic British could possibly make it work. The result is itself a compromise. On the one hand, anybody is free to expound reforming doctrine; on the other, politicians and administrators are secure in the knowledge that the practicalities of implementing change will always stop reform well short of revolution. It is in the nature of governmental systems to be, consciously or unconsciously, more interested in stability than in advance; and the more complex the society becomes the greater need it feels to concentrate on keeping itself going. Thus in Britain in recent years we have seemed to need a war to produce a major change in educational policy, such as those ushered in by the great Acts of 1902, 1918 and 1944. Perhaps, as economics replaces religion and social class as the main determinant of educational provision, entry to the European Economic Community may provide the required stimulus for the next. It certainly seems that for us some external force is needed to break down, even temporarily, our preoccupation with maintaining stability.

'Belief in the stable state is central, because it is the bulwark against the threat of uncertainty,' as Dr Donald Schon said in the first of his 1970 Reith Lectures. This is the era of ecology, the study of organisms in relation to environment, the science of interrelationships. We can no longer profitably discuss our world and its future in simple linear terms—progress; challenge and response; thesis, antithesis, synthesis —for the evidence all around us is of multi-dimensional, complex interactions. We can no longer welcome all change as beneficial (or likely to lead by subsequent reverse to benefit). We need to consider carefully what its effects might be.

Now it is clearly all to the good that we should recognise that progress is not an automatic God-given right flowing automatically from any change. The trouble is that this recognition is often indistinguishable in practice from merely justifying the *status quo*. So it is not surprising if we become restless with a system that is better at not changing than at changing, and if much of the debate about the planning of education focuses on whether the present system with its checks and balances has to be retained, as an essential of democracy, or whether more centralisation would get better results.

The argument, in terms of planning, is, I suggest, of minor importance. All organisations tend to be more concerned with, and better suited to, performing the elaborate balancing act required to maintain stability than exploring the possibilities of change. And since this exploration is fundamental to the planning process, adjustments of the organisation pattern tend to be, in relation to planning, transitory and superficial. From this angle neither the present arrangements nor new ones with more centralised power seem adequate to tackle the special planning problems of education.

The present system is a kind of compromise machine. People often explain it as a partnership, notably between the Department of Education and Science, the local authority (LEA) and the teacher. It is a homely metaphor. We are invited to think of three chaps amicably chewing over problems together, a sort of family situation in which, though power is not equally distributed, everyone at least has a voice. In reality, interplay of these three abstractions is utterly unlike that of independent individuals. For instance, the DES is only part of a government; the LEA, one of several score anyway, embraces both council and education committee; the teacher is a member of a union and an employee of the LEA as well as one of a staff serving under a head, or a head trying to lead a staff. And, of course, there are many other sophistications attached to the role of each 'partner', not to mention many other partners (such as the voluntary bodies, the universities and even the poor old parents).

Administratively, the arrangements seem to reflect adequately the pattern of life in our kind of society. From a planning point of view, however, the metaphor loses some of its appeal. Since the turn of the century when the partnership began its slow painful birth there have been enough changes to warrant drastic rethinking about the concept with its implications of *ad hoc*, compromise solutions and internal dissensions. For instance, the status of education, the esteem in which it is held and its perceived value have increased, and in consequence more and more money has been ploughed into it. There is a strong case for planned deployment of resources of a more sophisticated kind than the partnership could hope to achieve. Naturally, many people have concluded that the answer is to give greater powers to the central government.

Their argument gains no support from the evidence of recent history. The central government has removed over the years more and more power from the local authorities. Yet, on examination, it seems scarcely to have put this power to positive use, but has rather increased its negative control. For example, the 1944 Act left the form of secondary education to the LEAs. The government of the day declared its intention in 1965 to introduce comprehensive education. This, theoretically, was a shift of power to the centre. But this intention was, and could only be, implemented by negative methods—refusal to allow LEAs to build secondary schools that did not conform to this aim. That, and exhortations, was as much as the government could achieve before going out of office in 1970 (when its successors promptly removed the deterrent).

The vacuum at the centre

The central government, in our society, is in practice subject to many of the same constraints as other agencies. Thus significant changes in educational policy are usually only announced after a representative advisory committee has produced a report on the situation. This process evoked a caustic comment from John Lello who characterised the advisory committee report as a counter in an organisation game, as an example, in fact, of the increasing—and increasingly negative—power of the central government.*

> They can initiate, implement, forget, and shelve. Perhaps their greatest power is to acknowledge the existence of a problem, convene a committee, discuss a report, and then ignore the proposals. This power to ignore can be the most crucial weapon, since for many, the fight involved in discussion leaves the warrior too exhausted to fight for action. In this way a government is able to sidetrack positive decisions.

Lello went on to suggest a more courageous centralisation as a remedy:

> Ultimately the problem which is revealed is not to discover who takes the decisions but to investigate why so few decisions are taken at all. The effective barrier caused by the fear of increased centralisation has accounted for some of the inherent brinkmanship which characterises the lack of initiative from the central government. Perhaps the time has come to look more carefully at other countries and evaluate their different approaches as a proof that many of our traditional fears are groundless, and as an incentive to achieve more for British education.

However, attempts at greater central planning and control so far have not been encouraging—nothing like the crisp decision-making,

* *The Official View of Education*, Oxford: Pergamon, 1964.

free from extraneous clutter, envisaged by its advocates. For one thing, the extraneous clutter resists being swept away: educational institutions may vociferously invoke academic freedom when an attempt is made to control their funds or plan their intake; local councils, particularly those of the opposite party to the government, make mighty noises about dictatorship when any standardisation measure is proposed.

We have grown used to these phenomena. Recently, though, a new (and therefore much more alarming) one has arisen. The much greater susceptibility of central government in the 1960s to influence from pressure groups represents a bigger threat to constructive planning than the reactions of the other partners in the governmental process, because these reactions can be expected and allowed for whereas the influence of pressure groups is essentially arbitrary. The accessibility of central government to pressures and the effectiveness of the pressure groups is well illustrated by the effect of the mass media of communication, and notably television.

Instant news and instant comment, the instant presentation of highly dramatised issues—all this creates a climate in which anything but an instant response can be made to look like shifty evasion; hence the fashion for instant government. Television puts a premium on slickness of response by politicians almost, it sometimes seems, regardless of its relevance.

For this we have to thank its voracious appetite for material, for round-the-clock coverage, for novelty and sensation. This is what in the end makes the pressure group pattern arbitrary. The most carefully planned campaign for a wage claim, or a reform, or the ending of some real or imagined evil, can fall flat if its climax coincides with a Peruvian earthquake or a Pakistan flood. What matters for governments that wish to retain the confidence of the people, it seems, is that they must be ready to react quickly to whatever turns up. If a man can be there with a camera in a few minutes, the implication is, then the authorities should have been able to solve the problem and have a prepared statement ready.

In these circumstances the *ad hoc* can easily be elevated to the status of a philosophy, and this is the antithesis of planning. Of course, television is ultimately not the cause of this but a symptom. The chief danger of greater central government control in our kind of capitalist democracy with its ambivalent producer–consumer relationship is not that of iron-handed dictatorship but of a *Wizard of Oz* situation where, after all the searching for the ultimate source of power, a frightened little man cowers behind the imposing facade. In a modern version of *The Wizard of Oz* he would doubtless, when discovered, be studying the results of an opinion poll.

The extent to which members of parliament should be—and are—

representatives of the people or merely delegates, is an interesting theoretical speculation. It would no doubt be possible to chart the changes at different periods as the pendulum has swung back and foward. One could note, too, the relative strengths at various times of Cabinet and House of Commons; and the extent to which separate ministries are free to pursue their own policies or are subject to co-ordination. Individual political leaders can, and, hopefully, will continue to, have an influence on events. But all these adjustments are more easily explained as aspects of the balancing act than of positive planning. There has been in recent years growing evidence that on major issues—think, for instance, of incomes and prices—we have created a policy-making vacuum in which the central government can do little more than shout into the echoing void.

The other partners

Can we look more optimistically, perhaps, towards strengthening the other partners' roles? What of the argument that so far from increasing central power we need to redress the balance, and that the reorganisation of local government by creating bigger, more powerful units, will do the trick? The phrase 'redress the balance' gives the answer. In terms of government and the balancing act such reform makes sense: in terms of educational planning it is likely to be largely irrelevant. I have suggested that amidst the increasingly intricate manoeuvres required to preserve governmental balance, arbitrariness can assert itself, and that arbitrariness is the enemy of planning. It appears to have been increasing locally as well as nationally so far as education is concerned. One reason is the gradual but unmistakable reduction of the powers of education committees in relation to local councils.

In this 1958 was a significant date. Until then there was a strong direct relationship between what is now the Department of Education and Science and local education committees. There was a percentage grant specifically for education from the government to the LEA so that there was an incentive to spend on approved educational projects and, conversely, the possibility of a reduction in revenue for a recalcitrant authority. This was admittedly a blunt instrument for planning purposes but it was sharper than any available after 1958 when the block grant (later the rate support grant) came in. From then on an overall sum went from the government to the council for it to distribute throughout its range of services.

Now this is a complicated matter and the precise effects of the change are still being hotly debated. In purely financial terms some have claimed that education has achieved the same share of what was available as it would have done under the old system. However, our concern is not simply with money but with the terms on which it is offered. In many places, for instance, more decisions affecting the education service were arbitrary because more were taken on the basis of standardisation throughout all local services. (Treating the education service like all the others sounds fair enough, and it often is, but it is a principle that tends to ignore not merely education's special pleading but also its special needs.) Then again the craftier pressure groups in education, sensitive to the shift in power, began to aim at the leaders of the council rather than of the education committee, at the clerk rather than the education officer.

Hard upon this change have come in many areas sweeping administrative changes that recognise the new financial realities, subordinating education committees and their officers to new kinds of overlordship. In this context the fact that as costs have mounted and educational aspirations have risen many authorities have been seen to be too small to function properly, assumes much less significance. The potential for constructive planning by LEAs in partnership with the education ministry envisaged by the 1944 Act is diminished when the direct line between the two is weakened and when both locally and centrally educational leadership is circumscribed.

It might be thought perhaps that the third main partner, the teachers, would have become stronger as a result of this. In a sense they have, in that consultation with teachers, on everything educational, has become a reality. But other forces have made the teacher's potential strength less than it could have been, chief amongst them specialisation. First, where once the teachers' responsibility for the child's education was all-embracing, it is now shared with a variety of other experts—psychologists, careers officers, youth officers and so on. Second, the teaching side of education has itself been subdivided over the years—into primary, secondary and further education, with smaller subdivisions within each sector. Recently the sectionalism this has produced has led to unconstructive tensions (for example, inter-union arguments over salaries) that have probably weakened the status of the profession as a whole, and certainly have made it less effective than it could have been in the context with which we are here concerned—that of positive planning for the education service.

In this context the increased participation of teachers that I have suggested as a fundamental seems unlikely to be achieved through the partnership. The multiplication of checks and balances within the ranks of teachers reflects the preoccupation of the partnership as a whole with stability and control. When these are the aims the resolution of tension between the demands of democracy and efficiency gives way to a convenient reciprocal arrangement: the many safeguards—governing bodies, divisional executives, education

B

committees, advisory committees and so on—that help to preserve academic freedom, also make it impossible for teachers to control the service. However desirable and effective this may be governmentally, in planning terms the result is a contribution to the policy vacuum.

Purpose in planning

It remains to be seen whether the partnership can generate enough power from within the service to create a major new education Act. Meanwhile the decline in its effectiveness since the magnificent achievements of the two decades following that of 1944 is plain to see. Planning initiative seems now to have passed outside the education service. Planning the economy, town and country planning and latterly planning the strategy of local authorities have all been taken up, and each has produced its specialists. Physical planners, treasurers with computers, and now programme planners, abound. In comparison the efforts of the education service to plan itself have seemed puny and amateurish. The education service is by now more planned against than planning.

This conforms to a fairly general pattern. Our technological achievements today have far outstripped our moral and social development. We have become so adept at making machines to do our work for us that in the social services we seem increasingly to create machinery and institutions instead of grappling with our fundamental problems. Planning by external management techniques is an aspect of this, as is our concentration on questions of organisation.

The techniques we apply to human activities should be firmly grounded in the fundamental principles underlying the activities if they are not to debase them. As handmaidens they can be immensely valuable: as prime movers they are dangerous, promising much but quickly leading to sterility. In particular they are likely to elevate smooth running far above its proper station in life: steady state becomes all-important and technological advance becomes self-sufficient.

This, then, is the core of the argument for a new kind of educational planning, one in which everyone engaged in the service, lay or professional, can participate, and one in which participation is meaningful. The conventional processes have largely concerned themselves with manipulating counters in an organisation game and have lost much of their value in educational policy-making, which is increasingly required to adapt itself to external circumstances.

In a system that shows every sign of preoccupation with preserving steady state, the new approach to planning must be radical and fundamentalist. Neither juggling with the balance of power nor improving technical and managerial wizardry will help unless we put ends before means. For this we have to begin by setting clear and precise objectives. It is in this basic activity that the participation of the practitioner can—and, for success, must—play a key part.

2 Education and the language of planning

The previous chapter argued that it is more important for the education service that we should change its approach to planning than its organisation. To suggest this is to shift the focus of attention from the structure of the service to its texture. In considering how those engaged in education can play a significant part in its planning we need to look at roles and relationships and at the context in which they operate. How well, for example, does the local government framework enable teachers to participate in planning?

The local government context

Local government is one of the favourite scapegoats for the defects in our educational provision. Much of the criticism is unfair and most of it unconstructive. Yet it seems broadly true that the esteem in which education is held tends to suffer because of its association with an institution the public appears to care little about. In higher education and amongst secondary schools there is a kind of caste system in which local authority control is an important dividing line. Nor has education much in common, either in its scale or in its nature, with many of its sister services: it is a stumbling-block for schemes of local government reorganisation.

Serious thinking about the role, as distinct from the organisation, of local authorities is long overdue. One fundamental question that might be asked is how appropriate today is the name local *government*. The side of councils' work concerned with actual government is small and diminishing: their main role is providing services as local interpretation of national policy. Yet the traditions and methods of local authorities are governmental. Consider, for instance, the problems attaching to the job of the elected councillor.

Part-time, unpaid status may have been entirely adequate when there was a good supply of leisured, public-spirited men of means available, when fewer attendances at meetings were required, and when services were less costly and complex. Today the nature of local government, more politically oriented, more demanding in time and knowledge, makes it unattractive to many and impossible for many more. Education committees, which are of course largely made up of councillors, are often in even worse straits than other committees. Because they are responsible for such a large amount of work over a wide range of institutions they tend to have many subcommittees: then, too, there are school and college governing and managing bodies, each with its quota of education committee members. So wanting to serve on the education committee tends to be a minority interest; and a willingness to become its chairman, with all the ancillary tasks peculiar to that office, may be rare indeed.

For those who do decide to serve, there are many frustrations and sources of confusion. Membership of policy-making bodies like education committees, and the traditional function of the councillor—safeguarding the rights of individuals, ensuring fair treatment and so on—both require very special gifts. A man is lucky, and unusual, if he has one of these: to look for both at once is to expect too much. Furthermore, the two roles may often clash.

If the two roles were separated it would be possible to broaden the base of education committee membership and thus strengthen it. As it is, councillor-members often have a well-nigh impossible task. Their traditional function of measuring professional proposals against their common sense on behalf of the electorate grows ever more difficult: the choice of saying 'yes' or 'no' to a highly specialised report is really no choice at all. And as members of councils seeking to weigh the claims of various committees (or their officers) against each other, their task is indeed thankless.

It is not to be wondered at if many councillors find themselves able to do little more than loyally support the broad political decisions of their parties. Nor is it then surprising if teachers, finding little sensitivity in this approach to their educational aspirations, should feel themselves in a dialogue of the deaf and yearn for different masters. Yet in many respects, councillors may be just as much prisoners in the system as their nominal employees.

It used to be widely believed that education officers were the captors, that they skilfully manipulated their committees under the guise of serving them. There is naturally a sense in which full-time permanent officials may always be expected to have a strong influence over part-time, temporary, elected representatives, but controversies like that over comprehensive education have shown teachers and the public that on major issues it is the basic political attitude of the council that counts. On these issues it may be very clear, too, that neither education committee members nor education officers have been able to ensure that educational merit has been the main criterion in decision-making. My concern here is not to argue that education should be freed from politics, for clearly it has very important political implications. It is to suggest that these spectacular glimpses behind the curtain are often indicators of a general pattern of decision-making in which there is far too little opportunity for educational questions to be discussed on educational grounds at levels at which resources are being allocated, and thus at which effective policy decisions are being made.

In this education is like the other social services. Of course the principle—that when a variety of claims are made on the public purse there has to be some method of evaluating them—is unexceptionable. When we examine the practice there may be much less justification. A common device is to set up special committees whose function is to control the expenditure and activities of the committees responsible for the various services and in effect to settle priorities. The officers and the committee members may be largely drawn from outside the ranks of those who provide the services.

The assumption is that neutrality, together with general managerial expertise, is the best standpoint for settling priorities. Now this may be a valid principle for industry or any enterprise in which there is no disagreement about values, or objectives, only about ways of achieving them, but its relevance to local government is minimal. For here we have a collection of heterogeneous social services with widely differing objectives; and how much money is given to them depends in the end on the value set on achieving the respective objectives of each one. To attempt this comparative evaluation without the involvement of those responsible for the services concerned is to invite dangerous over-simplification of the issues involved.

The inadequacy of the concept escapes notice in many authorities because the finance (or other senior) committee of the council concerns itself much more with allocating resources than evaluating or even questioning objectives. Specific instances of policy are put forward by the service-providing committees and these are judged individually on their merits. Attempts at comprehensive reviews of policy by education committees are rare, and if they are carried out they tend not to be submitted to the finance committee.

This means that the process by which objectives are determined is detached from that by which resources are allocated. We shall look at some of the effects of this in a later chapter: here the point to be made is that this elevates opportunism far above its station. It is another aspect of arbitrariness, negating the planning process, for the specialists are encouraged to base their case on what they think might find favour with those who hold the purse-strings rather than on what their service chiefly needs.

In this, elected members, administrators and teachers are all equally affected. Because the process tends to be arbitrary, through its inevitable insensitivity to the nuances of educational values, the result is usually not so much a tyranny as another instance of a policy vacuum. Those submitting proposals, for instance, usually have ways and means of concealing information that might weaken their case, or of acquiring more resources than they strictly need for certain projects likely to be favoured by the hierarchy, in order to set aside a little for others that may not be so popular. And when the various factions feel that they are on different sides in the exercise there can never be the thorough and honest appraisal nor the full co-operation that successful planning needs. So the outcome may be a compromise, or more accurately, a draw, for the process is in effect a contest.

These superficially unpromising circumstances may actually provide fruitful soil in which the seeds of better planning can be sown. Teachers, together with education officers and committee members, may be able to take the initiative by creating an approach based on analysis of the service that they, and only they, fully know. At best this might produce more compelling arguments for increased resources to undertake educationally desirable projects: at worst it would, by helping to avoid waste, enable better use to be made of what resources there are. A prerequisite of this initiative is to solve a communication problem, to develop a common language for those who work in education.

A common language

Expertise, whether that of the practitioner or the administrator, tends to produce its own characteristic language. Unfamiliarity with that language is one of the main reasons why experts reject or despise the opinions of outsiders, those who are laymen to them. Thus sometimes, regrettably, education officers and teachers may seem to have not too high an opinion of the intelligence of the committee members with whom they come into contact. Often this simply means they do not agree with their political views or social attitudes or that they have had cherished proposals turned down; but frequently it is because the professionals mistake for obtuseness the amateurs' natural unfamiliarity with matters to which the experts devote their lives.

The point is illustrated by the fact that some experts believe that professional colleagues in other disciplines are not very bright either. Experts develop their own short-cuts of thought and speech, their own jargon, as an industrial language, and they find it difficult to accept the opinions of those who are not fluent in their own particular jargon as being of equal value to their own. A common planning language between teachers and administrators, and one that would also be meaningful to the intelligent layman, would be an important advance.

At first sight, the omens are not good. In education, as in other social services, emphasis on organisation has tended to place a greater value on co-ordination than on field-work, and has given a superior status to the language of co-ordinators, a language that stems from those who co-ordinate the co-ordinators. (In local government this means clerks and treasurers, town managers and so on, who co-ordinate the activities of education and other social service officers, who co-ordinate those of teachers and other field-workers.)

Thus the basic speech of education offices tends to be very different from that of schools and colleges, even though most senior education administrators are recruited from teaching. Building codes, committee procedures, articles and instruments of government, scholarship regulations and so on have little in common with the curricula, disciplinary and pastoral themes of common rooms. Although superficially this may seem entirely appropriate, it may well be that of the two dialects, that of the education office is on examination the more peripheral: its preoccupation is with administration, with institutional management rather than planning.

Indeed there are signs that this is being recognised. Things are changing and the way this is happening is most significant, and very hopeful, for the notion of a common planning language, at least within education. Initiatives are beginning to come from the academic world, which suggests that the notion of teachers as key figures (instead of lookers-on) may be realistic rather than starry-eyed.

Our attitudes towards both education and administration are changing. In education, the old hierarchy of studies—pure science; applied science; social 'science'—has taken a jolt, notably of course from potential students: the social sciences, as ecology emerges as a core discipline, are beginning to come into their own as the most convincing interpreters of our complex interacting universe; applied science thrusts itself forward as people demand a relevant education. In administration, academic distinction, preferably in classics, is no longer automatically assumed to be the ideal preparation, nor are the cool judgments it is said to facilitate always thought entirely adequate for a world that will not stand still long enough for judgments to be handed down. The new perspectives required by administrators are similar to those needed by schools.

Significantly, educational administration in Britain is beginning to mean more nearly what it means in the United States: that is, not something for the folk in the office nor a fancy name for drawing up the timetable, but the managerial function of heads, principals and academics as well as those at headquarters. For one thing, the growth of colleges and large secondary schools has compelled even the most obstinate pragmatists to begin to master the arts and sciences of management: sometimes big institutions in small authorities have set the pace for the area.

But beyond this there are clear signs that teachers and traditional administrators are beginning to feel the need for a new philosophical framework. Such a framework, in which organisation and methods are not just techniques but the skeleton of a sensitive, interacting system, in which communications science is not just a desirable extra but an acknowledgment of our need to interpret our world ecologically, seems every day more clearly to be the best hope of tightening our uncertain grasp on life's controls.

For we must acknowledge that any attempt to discover or to order information today has to come to terms with ecology, which is emerging as a fundamental, unifying discipline. If we seek insights into complex interrelationships, such as the microcosm in which school, neighbourhood, parent and teacher interact with the child, we are beginning to see that we must do so within the ambience of a greater world of resources and needs, of race, class, work, urbanisation, and the elemental challenge of climate.

Let us be clear, too, that so far as teachers are concerned these are essentials not merely to spin the wheels of our growing educational institutions, but to inform and sensitise the teaching process itself. If we look at the major influences that are transforming our view of education we shall find there is a common theme. In the next few pages I shall refer briefly to a few of these influences before turning to the question of whether educators can use an approach based on this common theme to rescue the planning process from a decline into sterility.

Influences on education

The central development in pedagogy itself, one that has been going on for over half a century, is that which emphasises learning rather than teaching, education rather than instruction. The story of this movement, from learning-through-activity-and-experience to curriculum development, is too familiar to need elaboration here: we must, however, notice that throughout it lays great stress on the notion of relevance to life.

This is one of the main reasons why the social sciences, psychology and sociology, are now so prominent in the training of teachers. Sociology is currently the most spectacular and perhaps the most profound influence on education. It provides a systematic framework for asking neglected but fundamental questions like what a school is for and what education actually does in a society; it can present the education service as a social system and the school as a sub-system, so illuminating roles and relationships. It puts education in context, showing how the curriculum and methods can only be fully effective if they are related to this setting and, therefore, how educational innovation must be planned in relation to it. A growing number of teachers use the perceptions of sociology either consciously or intuitively to help them do their day-to-day classroom jobs properly.

(In both curriculum development and the application of the social sciences the attempt to explore the implications, systematically, of the notion of relevance to life seems, incidentally, to illustrate similarities between the needs of the educational and of the planning process. There is, for instance, the realisation that there is no standard learning process, but that different strategies may be needed for learning the various things that come under the umbrella-term 'education': in learning as in planning we may be dealing with a wide range of different but related objectives which need to be identified before we begin.)

Another fundamental is the notion of active response by the learner, leading to the concept of programmed learning in which individuals can pace themselves. It is now widely accepted that this is an important key to the operation of any system to which information is introduced. Its acceptance in education does not merely call for new techniques—although these are needed: a much more profound effect is that producing programmes not only demands new skills but a rethinking of aims and attitudes.

These attitudes are implicit in the recent development of educational technology in which the great variety of teaching machinery and audio and visual equipment, including film, radio and television, is considered as a whole, as a means of devising strategies for education, choosing the appropriate medium for particular, carefully thought-out elements of the total process.

Another challenge to preconceptions comes when computers are amongst the media concerned. Computer-assisted education uses them to set tests, detect errors and help to correct them. Though it is scarcely yet capable of widespread implementation the idea clearly illustrates two things. The first is that psychologists, teachers and electronics engineers have combined their skills to develop new ways of teaching which (over a surprisingly large area of operation) are more rigorous and more thorough than those of the unassisted human and may even have more regard for the needs of the individual. The second is that electronics offers a more sensitive approach to automation than the purely mechanical one—the distinction between man and machine which once seemed so rigid has been eroded, resulting in a major breakthrough in the potentialities of learning. We are beginning to accept that in many aspects of life, those in which the interrelationship of cause and effect is most complex, the best tools for understanding are computers. And, of course, these aspects include the most important and difficult sides of our life, such as decision-making.

Few individuals could hope to master all these recent extensions of the teacher's role, so collective approaches are increasingly used. Team-teaching aims at combining the resources of people each talented in particular ways—some technically minded, some patient expositors, some good group discussion leaders and so on. (Significantly, this co-operative approach is also the characteristic method of one of the most important planning developments of our time, operational research, about which we must say more later.)

Yet the co-operation itself can scarcely take place without some common attitudes, some unifying influence on the participants. Without it, all the new developments will seem to be separate, with the danger that each one may seem to some to be a panacea and to others a gimmick, whereas they should be regarded as parts of a whole. We need a conceptual framework that will fuse all the new disciplines.

Systems thinking

If we are to go beyond simply enriching a basically unchanged style of teaching by these new developments, we have to consider them together, and how they relate to each other. There are the possibilities in audio-visual equipment, programmed learning and, perhaps, computerisation. There are the prospects of curriculum development. There are new teaching techniques. There is the need to see education as a social process. They present several possible ways to achieve the same educational end and the question arises of finding the most effective one, not just once and in theory but regularly and in practice. Add the need to consider the resources available—money, men, buildings and equipment—and we have a problem that even the finest intuition cannot be sure of solving.

Nor can any individual discipline cope with them all. In response to this felt need, then, what is known as the systems approach has been developed. It is not itself a discipline, like mathematics or Greek, but an approach, an application of a concept. Thus we can talk of systems engineering, systems learning or systems analysis in referring to particular applications.

The next chapter will briefly consider some of these in relation to educational and other social planning. It will argue that the needs of the educational process and the needs of its planning are such that a transformation based on a systems approach is necessary and is possible. Such an approach, by relating the educating and planning functions, may serve as a unifying discipline in teaching and as a means whereby teachers may assume a central role in planning.

3 Systems and education

To describe living beings in physical and chemical terms is to omit half the picture. What is left out is the relationship between the parts that somehow injects purpose into them. This same factor of relationship is what distinguishes a mere collection of phenomena from a system. A system might be described as an array of things in which we are concerned particularly with the way they relate to, and interact with, each other. Systems analysis is a method of understanding the way a system works preparatory to influencing or controlling it.

In this chapter the systems approach will be considered as it relates to social planning. In exploring its processes of understanding, controlling and communicating, we shall look at distinct but related disciplines as aspects of the common language and also at the interrelationship between education and planning.

Understanding and control

Before control, then, comes the attempt to understand how systems work. In this, if the specific application is to social planning, the logical starting-point is sociology. Some idea of the specific contribution of systems theory to sociology may come from comparing the approach of an early formative influence on the development of organisation theory, Max Weber, with more recent approaches. Weber emphasised the 'purely technical superiority' of bureaucratic administration 'over any other form of organisation'. 'Precision, speed, unambiguity, knowledge of the files, continuity, discretion, unity, strict subordination, reduction of friction and of material and personal costs—these are raised to the optimum point.'*

The basis of this view is the theory of division of labour, dating back to Adam Smith's *Wealth of Nations* in the eighteenth century. Weber's application of it to administration generally, not just to industrial production, marked a step forward, but subsequent analysis of the way organisations actually work has shown the need to allow for unplanned results, such as, for instance, the resentment and feeling of isolation that comes from fragmentation. Systems theory allows the possibility of unintended as well as intended consequences.

Amongst modern sociologists, Talcott Parsons has been highly influential in developing the notion of the system. He has examined specifically the element of social relationship in systems

* *From Max Weber*, trans. and ed. H. H. Gerth and C. Wright Mills, London: Routledge & Kegan Paul, 1948.

consisting of interacting persons: society as a whole, then, as sub-systems, such things as committees and families.* What Parsons calls 'the paradigm of social interaction' has been the key to better understanding of a wide range of social institutions.

Education can be (and, of course, nowadays frequently is) studied as a social system, with the school as a significant sub-system. From such studies we can better understand and perhaps better weigh the value of its processes and events: we can for example discover this way its implicit values and priorities and thus find out about possible social biases. The face-to-face encounter of teachers representing one sub-culture and children representing another is an interaction only now starting to move from the unconscious and unreflecting sphere to that of the conscious and aware: understanding of this process, amongst the most crucial for the future development of education, is one of the fruits of systems analysis.

Systems, viewed sociologically, are clearly highly complex. When analysis seems to reveal simpler systems then it appears correspondingly easier to move through the stage of understanding to that of controlling. An interesting example is that of economics. An organised system can be considered as an economy, its parts interrelating to assess the availability of resources and to deploy them. Recently special attention has been given, in micro-economics and econometrics, to the way this operates in industry and the public services. Education has thus been greatly influenced by economic thought. Indeed, the policy vacuum has to a considerable extent been filled by acceptance of the implicit objectives that have arisen from using industry as a model for understanding the education service.

Thus a recent (and very good) book on higher education, *The Impact of Robbins* by Layard, King and Moser,† begins: 'Apart from electronics and natural gas higher education has grown faster than any major national enterprise in the 1960s'; and a dozen lines later we find: 'How has this fantastic explosion come about? . . . like so many things, this question is best looked at in terms of demand and supply.' The authors describe the situation in now-familiar terms:

People seek education both for its own sake as a form of 'consumption', and as an 'investment' providing the means to a higher income. As a good in itself, education is felt to add to the interest and grace of life; and when people get richer they seek more of it, just as they buy more novels or hi-fi sets. The education of a child places heavy costs on his family in terms of loss of earnings, even if tuition is free. And, as living standards rise, people can more easily afford to meet these costs, just as

* See, for example, *The Social System*, Chicago: The Free Press, 1951.
† Harmondsworth: Penguin, 1969.

they can afford more of other forms of 'consumption'. But people also want education as a way to better-paid jobs. And as a country grows richer, the labour market's demand for educated people rises relative to the demand for those with lesser skills—much of modern capital equipment can only be used by educated workers and so on. As a result the number of people for whom education can be financially profitable increases steadily, and more seek to be educated.

As an interpretation of a prevailing contemporary attitude towards education this is just, but as an underlying philosophy for a vital social process it seems inadequate. If it were a comprehensive analysis of cause and effect in education, perhaps controlled growth to the benefit of the whole community would be a more immediate prospect than it seems, in fact, to be. Profit—even 'profit' so liberally interpreted as to encompass the fringes of altruism—is not so consistently acceptable to mankind as a motive that it can become a basis for planning. It flies in the face of human biology in too many ways. The analysis needs, it seems, to be more sophisticated. When this need is acknowledged, economics no longer appears quite so ready an instrument of control. For one thing, it is beset by its own basic notion of balance and imbalance. Economic growth has a seemingly inherent tendency to be inconsistently distributed: some areas grow faster than others; new industries overtake others; towns do better than country and so on. And it seems as though this cannot be controlled by direct human agency such as government action. Long-term economic programmes have never been successful in Britain at imposing themselves on events, only at best and marginally in short-term reactions to the swings and upsets of events.

Can we look, then, to a more subtle instrument of understanding, and thus of control, in political science? As the setting of standards is a key factor in this it seems a more promising approach. A political system is one concerned with the relationships that society regulates by exercising public power, either centrally or through some agency. The relationships in question may be those between such things as exports and imports, houses and homeless, sickness and treatment. The control is sought through setting standards: in education, for instance, in order to fix rates for student grants we must have standards of subsistence. The standards we need have to be based on principles that take a flexible view of human nature (more so than economics, for instance) both in its inconsistency and in its potentiality.

As to the inconsistency, political systems are well able to accommodate it. The range of relationships to be regulated is not only variable between different societies but may—and frequently does—change within particular societies. Thus the relationship between men and their earnings has recently been moved in and out of the public sector. So far as the potentiality is concerned, political action has been the route by which men have made most social progress in modern times. Individuals may be reluctant to perform disinterested acts of their own volition but they are often willing to assent to political action that benefits others rather than themselves. This is one reason why politics is so often described as the art of the possible.

In comparing the application to social questions of political science with that of economics I am not seeking to present them as competing disciplines. In systems terms they are complementary facets of one basic process: the point is simply that the one must, at certain critical points, be considered within the context of the other. To take a comparable example from industry, the concepts of systems engineering are not invalidated by the development of ergonomics.

Systems engineering arose from the need to deal quickly with increasingly complex problems of design in engineering. The approach was to define precisely the objectives of the system to be designed and all later design decisions were rigorously subordinated to them. Next it meticulously indicated what each part of the system had to do before making assumptions about how best to achieve these objectives; and it completed this process for the whole of the system, considering it *as* a whole.

Yet, because of the very success of this approach in improving technology, and technological systems, the need has been felt for a sister science, ergonomics, the study of the human and non-human constituents of industry. Its alternative name, human engineering, is misleading with its suggestion of turning men into machines. In fact it applies social science findings to ways of suiting jobs to people. Using the principles—first things first, assume nothing, consider the whole—of the systems approach, it explores the potentialities of both man and machine and plans the function of each to best effect. Again the disciplines are complementary.

Of course, the greater the element of human involvement the more sophisticated the analysis of the system needs to be and the more difficult becomes the question of setting standards as a method of achieving control. We can illustrate the point by comparing control in engineering with that of political government. In one case the controller watches instruments which record variables, showing how they reach, overstep or fall below standards—like for instance the temperature gauge in one's car—and the signals he gets tell him what to regulate. Sophisticated systems can be made to regulate themselves and all are designed to be controlled. The statesman, politician or political scientist is differently placed. His system was not designed to be controlled by him; his signals have to try to predict what will happen without any certainty that human behaviour, unlike the behaviour controlling a temperature gauge, can be predicted; he has to set his own standards of what is the desirable level of regulation, or negotiate them with the people for whose welfare he has responsibility.

Control and communication

So, in social matters, questions of control cannot be separated from those of communication. Consider the ever-growing volume of relationships we want to regulate and the escalating standards we apply. To do this we need a vaster and vaster scale of operations, with more and more agreement from the governed and more and more time to carry it out. Yet the increasing pace of change gives us less and less time, for it constantly creates new situations which make the old standards obsolete and which increase the likelihood of unpredictable consequences through the great number of interactions they produce.

And all the time the basis of reaching agreement is weakened: by the maze of technicalities and interactions (how many people know enough about the implications of joining the Common Market to express a useful opinion on it?); by the equation of democracy with counting heads and the consequential vulnerability of the politicians to activist self-seeking minorities. And the time for fixing appropriate standards becomes less, not greater, as innovations may become obsolete before they can be implemented, like the kind of aircraft we nowadays design and cannot afford to produce.

Inextricably linked with the question of control, then, is that of communication. The interchange of information, another name for the learning process, is at the heart of all problems of planning and government. We can illustrate the point if we look at the process from a systems viewpoint.

In the hierarchy of systems that the universe embodies, even the most rudimentary are dynamic, not static. An object, however minuscule, exists in an environment and in time. It is better described as a phenomenon, not just an object but an event, the interaction of object and environment in time. Organic systems (and some inorganic ones) are open; that is, they interchange energy and matter with their environment. And the higher the level of the system the greater and the more complicated is this interaction; for higher systems are open to information as part of the interchange with the environment.

In fact, even at very low levels an organic entity uses information to regulate the way it itself is made up internally. But at the level that concerns us, organisms have developed means of using information in order to relate to and regulate the outside world.

Between human beings this highly important process is an interaction which we call communication; and the complicated patterns of interaction in society form a communications network. This communication, which is so critically important to us, has been created in certain inorganic systems, too. Automatic piloting, rocketry and certain kinds of industrial automation can perform the three main functions of the human mind: they are programmed to detect what is relevant to their objective, to evaluate it and to take appropriate action. If we apply this model to a social system we would expect the continual operation of the process to produce steady state; and this in a somewhat more elaborate way is what appears to happen. The only kind of variation we can envisage seems to occur if the social system itself is seen as part of something bigger. Most of the age-old philosophical and religious questions about the nature of man are in fact questions about whether we can see the whole scene. Accepting this limitation we cannot be certain about the direction of our universe, if any, or about the nature of man.

Man's interactions with environment and with time are highly complex, including irreversible change: although we counteract age collectively (by creating babies) we do not seem to be able to do so individually (by rejuvenation for instance). Man's communal dealings—with each unit operating individually as well as socially—are equally hard to puzzle out in terms of cause and effect, because of the interaction we call communication. The information we take in collectively and individually includes unconscious as well as conscious influences. The parallel with automated systems is more helpful in some ways than simple, biological explanations of man, such as the evolutionary view. From this angle he is a unit, at first largely programmed and later part-programmed part-programming, in a self-programming network.

One of our newer sciences, cybernetics, is concerned with these twin questions of control and communication. The pattern relates again to steady state (homeostasis), the kind of self-regulating mechanism that comes from feedback: like, for example, the automatic response of the car-driver to the deviations caused by the bumps in the road acting on his wheels, in order to keep the machine going straight. Cybernetics is concerned with humans, with machines, and with social systems of learning and consequent behaviour. It relates information theory to goal-seeking, so that in a cybernetic system there is a selector to arrive at a goal, a detector supplying information about the world outside and an effector to carry out the action.

Here we approach the essence of systems theory—the perception of certain common principles in all material systems, principles, that,

C

for example, cut across conventional notions of living creatures and machines. The basic distinction between these systems is whether they are open or closed: in closed systems, exchange of elements and energy with environment is limited and temporary, whereas in open systems there is characteristically continuous or regular exchange with the environment. Living organisms are open systems but not all open systems are living. This is not the right place—and I am certainly not the right person—to embark on detailed discussion of such profundities. But we can usefully notice that feedback, in man-made machines and in organisms, is a matter of similar structural arrangements. Significantly, in cybernetics the model is biological, not mechanistic. The subtle processes perceived and the speed of reaction needed, and the concepts of balance, control, communication and feedback, provide a more useful way of thinking about people, organisations and planning than a strictly engineering model.

From all this, from the confluence of all these ideas, comes perhaps our best hope of a common language. General systems theory is the basis for studying phenomena from many kinds of system. The imagination is perhaps entitled to boggle a little at the thought of the general systems conjurer trying to keep all those balls in the air. But it is not quite as bad as that. The approach in all these disciplines is strikingly similar, and general systems theory—wisely, you may think—does not try to conscribe all knowledge, but rather to apply the systems approach to particular problems wherever they may arise, seeking by the potentiality of the common language to investigate all ramifications from all possible angles. For example, education can be considered as a system, with schools and colleges as sub-systems operating within an environment, requiring information and using feedback; and the same analysis will serve whether the application is one of sociology, learning or building design.

The key role of education

In essence the systems approach represents a view that the elements of an organisation, because of the many variables in it—of men, technical content, methods, information, materials and so on—have a large number of potential relationships to each other, but that study of these relationships can tease out the best possible pattern.

We should be clear, however, that the promise of the systems approach is not simply that of helping us to understand how the pieces of our society fit together. The hope is that it can enable planning to encompass the element of purposeful innovation that distinguishes it from mere tinkering with organisational balance. In applying it to educational planning we are pursuing what seems to be our best chance of making progress with the creation of a society that is just and humane and at the same time stimulating and satisfying. We are seeking the way out of a dilemma.

The philosophical landscape of the later twentieth century is far from easy on the eye. Much of it looks bleak and sterile. The emptiness of its vast barren tracks is relieved—if we except a few candy-striped popular side-shows—only by the wreckage of noble and optimistic Victorian concepts such as progress, creative evolution and scientific mastery of the universe. We have rightly rejected one-dimensional interpretations of life with their facile assumption that change leads to advance. But the subtler multi-dimensional interactions revealed by ecological studies can lead to thoroughly dispiriting interpretations.

Preoccupation with preserving steady state is for most people in the end unsatisfying. Yet it fills more and more of our lives. The population explosion, aided by the ability of advanced medical science and quick food distribution to keep people alive, has become our greatest contemporary problem. Overcrowding also helps our other modern enemies, violence and pollution. We have somehow to regulate these horrors or we can expect a cataclysmic event or series of events to restore the balance for us.

Yet planning that offers the prospect of shaping the destiny of human beings and their environment tends to be viewed with suspicion, at least in the Western world. We are rightly sceptical of claims by other people, however well-intentioned, to know what is best for us. We are beginning to be made aware of the extra hazards life has for the submerged millions who have to come to terms with a world structured for them by the favoured few. Planning that, consciously or unconsciously, has no loftier objective than preserving stability, merely strengthens this built-in bias.

The importance of education in helping us to break out of this vicious circle is that it offers the hope of helping people to control their own destinies and to do so responsibly. It offers, too, the hope of a nobler ideal than the stable state. Human beings need these ideals whether they can be justified logically or not. They need the prospect of better things. The old philosophical theories based on evolutionary patterns may today seem naïve, but their hearts were in the right place.

This can also be said of the—largely unspoken—philosophy of our education service. Whatever their other differences, almost all of those who work in it share an essentially optimistic outlook. Today more than ever the educational process has a central significance for mankind. In looking at the relevance of systems theory to education we are concerned to see not simply how much it may explain or unravel problems—we do not want a more sophisticated recipe for steady state—but also how it may help us to assert positive control over them.

In systems terms, human society is an open system into which information comes as a result of a complex process of the kind sociologists call socialisation—an absorption of culture, though it is by no means passive, as the phrase may seem to suggest. It is in fact a reciprocal process in which the context is also modifying itself by the fact of being a context (with the result that a lot of interrelated contexts are continually modifying themselves and each other). Assuming that our vision is clear, even thus far, we must accept the distinct possibility that if we could see further the new perspective might well alter our interpretation. That we have seen so far (and no further) is perhaps one of the main causes of our present unhappiness and anxiety. If we belonged to a society whose context (religious, economic, social) was clear, unambiguous and acceptable to all of its members, we should be spared much of the uncertainty that dominates our lives. Even the rebellious might find such a society more comfortable, for dissent becomes more meaningful and so more satisfying if it is dissent from something widely accepted rather than from a dissenting society. For us, 'change' or 'not change', rather than 'this kind of society' or 'that kind of society', is what we chiefly dispute.

The challenge for us is that we need a coherent and long-lasting context in order to focus, as we must, on values instead of unevaluated innovation. Yet the context must not come by the short-cut of imposed values. We are properly suspicious of the inroads of even relatively small (political, commercial, religious) attempts at what we justly call brain-washing. If there is a way out of this dilemma it seems most likely to come (a) by beginning with a smaller canvas than the whole social scene and (b) by a process that enables the perception of values rather than seeks to impose them. Education—of the right sort—could be that way out.

We rightly shrink from thoughts of positively introducing elements into the learning system that would seek to adjust social processes; but we have to take into account that the perpetuation of the *status quo*—which is the likely outcome unless we do positively try to adjust it—is in itself an indoctrination. It seems essential to build in the possibility of change: but change alone, unevaluated, is not enough. The evaluation is the difficult part: who is to do it and how? The present consensus style of government achieves, and seeks to achieve, no more than steady state. But the requirements for education are surely different from those for society as a whole: it is our best hope of eventually learning how to make value judgments about the way we live.

We must set free our education service at least from the sterile circular argument. Its purpose is to enable judgments to be made, not to impose them. It is an enabling service supporting an enabling process. If we consider the basic classroom process as an encounter between open learning systems, those of the teacher and the pupils, if we consider schools, colleges and universities as collections of these learning systems interacting with each other, with society and with other social processes, then there is no threat to the principles of democracy in the notion of the teacher accepting the responsibility of helping people to make value judgments.

Teachers as policy-makers

This concept sees educating as a form of planning, and the planning of education is in need of the same underlying approach as educating. It offers the prospect of a style of planning that will enable everyone, lay or professional, to play a part. It implies, furthermore, acceptance of the teacher in the role of policy-maker, key figure in planning.

This undoubtedly requires considerable readjustment of present attitudes about roles in educational planning, not least perhaps amongst teachers themselves. I have suggested earlier how essential this change is, and why; and later chapters will outline a suggested method.

In case this brief discussion of the systems approach may appear daunting, however, or seem suspiciously like the kind of wand-waving I specifically disavowed in the introduction, perhaps it might be as well to say a little about the essentially practical and utilitarian nature of the concept.

First, as to its practicability, we should be clear that nothing abstruse or esoteric is involved. Although systems thinking is capable of highly sophisticated development, in the present context it can best be considered as an ordered version of what we call common sense. It is concerned with fixing objectives, selecting appropriate means of achieving them, devising action programmes, assessing their impact and revising the process in the light of experience.

Second, we should be clear, too, that educators are in urgent need of such a tool for their basic function of educating. Their situation in relation to such new developments as those mentioned in the previous chapter is that of all specialists at the present time. The pressures of innovation, the new requirements for mastery of their disciplines, are unrelenting. Apart from the intrinsic challenge of new discoveries that may be made, there is the ever-present possibility that entirely new ways of looking at a problem may appear, so that currently accepted 'solutions', however perfect in themselves, may become obsolete. They may be by-passed, overtaken by new developments in other related disciplines about which the specialist—

beset amongst other difficulties by the growing time-lag in communications—may know nothing. Confronted by all these difficulties it is no use trying to combat them by acquiring more and more knowledge: what is needed is a method of approach that puts one's own specialism into context, and enables it to adapt itself to change.

Third, the kind of planning this approach engenders inevitably by its emphasis on objectives and evaluation moves the practitioner nearer the centre of the picture. As I shall hope to show in later chapters, we can develop, from the systems approach, ways of linking the process of allocating resources in local authorities—the traditional domain of finance committees—with the policy-making process of their education committees. But there is another kind of policy-making—again one that tends to operate in a vacuum—that of the teacher. He often makes policy collectively, at a staff meeting, in a teaching team, at a weekend course or in a curriculum development centre; and in front of his own pupils he is an individual policy-maker. What we call academic freedom is perhaps the most highly prized feature of our whole education system; but freedom from political or bureaucratic intervention also gives the freedom—and the obligation—to plan.

What, then, are the practical implications of this obligation? Amongst the policy-maker's tasks are these:

1 defining the problem;
2 thinking of possible ways of solving it; and
3 weighing the merits of the various ways, both in terms of quantitative assessments and of value judgments.

There are management tools to help him do this effectively, such as:

1 structuring problems—setting them out in an ordered fashion so as to see them more clearly;
2 considering problems in several dimensions—for example by using the multi-disciplinary approach of operational research; and
3 using models—that is, creating theoretical representations of a problem so as to try to predict what will happen in practice.

To be able to use these aids the specialist has to be prepared to see and express his discipline in wider terms, to use a common language. In this respect the requirements of educating and of planning education have basic similarities. A systems approach appears to offer a suitable conceptual framework for understanding the scope and nature of the problems involved in both.

4   Implications for administrative method

The systems approach with its initial emphasis on identifying objectives makes certain demands on administrators. It requires them to abandon, from time to time, the safe ground of building and managing institutions and step out into the unknown. For some this may mean a radical change of outlook. This chapter will consider some of the implications of the approach for administration.

What kind of administrators?

Educational administration means so many things to so many people that generalisation would be unprofitable. I have written elsewhere* about one aspect of administration, that of the LEA. Even in this limited field there is no recognisable style of administration. How could there be? The haphazard growth of education, the wide variety in size and sensitivity of the authorities, the enveloping traditions of controlling councils, the lack of agreement about educational aims—all these conspire against it.

The same is true of the many other types of educational administration. The universities, in so far as they have had a common policy, have seemed to restrict the activities of their professional administrators to the nuts and bolts of their machinery. In extreme cases they seem to make unreal distinctions between academic policy, axiomatically untouchable, and administration. Protocol amongst academics and the elaboration of procedures sometimes seem to be a major preoccupation. Creative management has scarcely caused a ripple on the surface of many universities.

The DES follows by and large the civil service method, itself now changing. 'Management' is becoming accepted as something heads of schools and colleges should know about—largely, at present, after they have been appointed, but with some indications that the need for relevant initial training may soon be more widely acknowledged. Approaches vary but generally tend, naturally enough in view of the stage of development we have reached, to be pragmatic. New institutions, such as the polytechnics, are beginning to make their own characteristic contribution. Local councils are experimenting, often borrowing ideas from industry, introducing new categories of administration that have, of course, an influence on the way education is managed.

* In *The Education Officer and His World*, London: Routledge & Kegan Paul, 1970.

There is growing awareness of the need for greater expertise in educational management, for a more thoroughgoing, less amateur approach. Characteristically, though, the situation tends to be viewed in organisational terms. Thus the fairly considerable extent of innovation in the titles and duties of new administrative appointments is not matched by a corresponding amount of analysis of the nature of the administration required. Many of the training courses now springing up probably reflect an underlying anxiety to probe this basic question, but the tradition of providing courses to produce personnel trained for specific, existing professional posts is strong and one should not expect too much trail-blazing from them.

The organisational aspects of the creation of effective administration are, of course, considerable. Local education officers, for instance, find themselves increasingly having to answer questions that in effect challenge their very existence. Is there any need any longer for a specifically educational bureaucracy at local level? Would not management men, using the resources and expertise of teachers more fully, be able to do the job now required much better? Are education officers who spring from the ranks of teachers likely to make the best contribution?

Then again, many people would argue that at present the education service is being fragmented, or threatened with fragmentation, by a number of developments—social work reorganisation, health service changes, regional control of advanced further education, community development. Education officers, they would say, are increasingly losing power to the local co-ordinators; their committees have less and less influence; the financial independence of the service has long gone.

In these circumstances many education officers are uncertain of what their role should be: ought they to align themselves with the teachers and become educational advisers to councils; or should they see themselves as potential town managers, bringing educational administration into line with that of other local services? Or is there, or could there be, a distinctive philosophy of educational administration, one that is more than an uneasy amalgam of educational thoughts and bureaucratic techniques?

These are, certainly, extremely important questions. In planning terms, however, they are not—or so it seems to me—the first questions that should be answered. However educational administrators are deployed, whoever employs them, whatever their list of duties contains, they all must face a much more basic challenge: whether or not their whole outlook may not be obsolete. This is a question that has to be faced by every manager who has reached, or is nearly reaching, middle age.

Perhaps every era is a critical one for the middle-aged; but our present one seems particularly crucial because of the pace of change and the impact of technologies. Young people—students, young executives, young teachers—are aware of the methods we need to bring decision-making under control. But older people tend to be sceptical or indifferent until they are personally affected, by which time it may be too late.

This is not, today, just a matter of differences of energy or of idealism between the young and the old, but the emergence of a whole style of thinking about life. The new sciences, conspicuously those of management and of society, and the technologies that go with them are not just desirable additions to our range of knowledge but our best hope of salvation.

So the implications of the systems approach to planning that we should chiefly consider relate to administrative method rather than to the deployment of administrators or even, initially, to their training. The foremost concern should not be with organisation. More than efficient machinery we need high-quality models to improve our understanding of the interrelated systems of the education service. We need, too, accurate projections of educational wants and educational needs. These are particularly necessary in a democratic service for it is these aspects of information that in effect replace the bureaucratic machinery, the largely one-way communicating links of insensitive systems.

They are needed in all parts of the service. For example, much depends on the approach of the central government administration. In a decentralised system such as ours we need stronger central administration, not weaker; stronger, that is, in promulgating what it cannot decree. Negative control is not enough: ways must be found of enabling and encouraging local advance. Equally, the two-way process of communication is incomplete if it stops abruptly at the headmaster's desk. Again, his first concern should be less with efficient machinery than with the interchange of ideas and information.

Any satisfactory planning process requires a sound basis of information on which value judgments can be based. Further, it needs rigorous self-analysis and testing of assumptions. The techniques we shall briefly consider now are not short-cuts to definitive answers but methods of undertaking this analysis. They concern us here only incidentally, but they may perhaps indicate the style of thought the contemporary administrator must cultivate in order to encourage effective planning. The references are necessarily brief, and are intended to do no more than illustrate this cast of thought more clearly than mere argument can do.

Techniques for systems

One of the characteristics of human beings is their ability to run things through in their minds without having to learn by physical trial and error (which can, of course, literally be fatal in relation to many problems). Theories are schematic representations, in the mind, of external phenomena: they may seek to explain or to predict. Many of the newer management techniques are attempts to take advantage of this ability, and to do so in an ordered fashion.

Any organisation that tries to assess itself or to amend itself in actual practice, as it goes along, is unlikely to get the best results and may meet disaster. An important aspect of management today

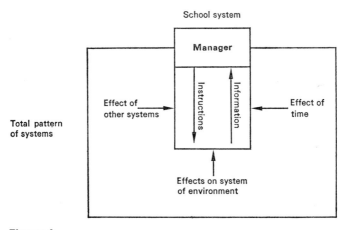

Figure 1

consists of creating theoretical models, functioning outside the operation of the organisation, that can replace, if they are good enough, some of the hazards of a purely pragmatic approach.

We can illustrate the point by thinking of our school or education authority as a system, inside other systems. Anyone trying to assess the school system while he is part of its normal operation encounters certain difficulties. Let us think, for instance, of the situation of anyone with managerial responsibilities in education: this might be illustrated as in Figure 1.

As the manager is himself a system within other systems his assessment is subject to the pressures of the environment and may therefore be distorted; and the unpredictable effects of external influences on the system, including time, may make the results of any review invalid. So he can make a model of, or simulate, the system outside the influences of environment; that is, in theory. Our diagram then takes on a different aspect (Figure 2). The results of the theoretical exercise in the simulated model can then be fed back into the operation of the real system.

Simulation is sometimes a theoretical representation of trial-and-error learning, a process by which we can run through possibilities in the mind rather than in actuality. (For this kind of simulation computers are increasingly used because they can run through many possible sets of circumstances much quicker than the human brain.) At other times a model is created that seeks to clarify the relationship

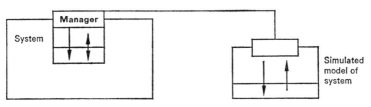

Figure 2

between component parts. Here the system being simulated is broken down into precisely indicated components: it is also to some extent stylised, that is to say stripped of inessentials. The aim is to simplify the actual pattern sufficiently for it to be understood: characteristically in this form of simulation only mathematics and its formulae can perform this service satisfactorily.

With complex human affairs, of course, stripping of inessentials can be a matter of opinion, so we need always to bear in mind the limitations, as well as the possibilities, of a strictly mathematical approach. Mathematics is to be regarded as a logical language devised to test certain hypotheses, not a means of creating assumptions. We have to remember, for example, that when the mathematician says, 'Let x equal the cost of closing a school,' he is assuming not only that there is such a cost but that it can be measured. Many of the important decisions in educational planning depend on probabilities not certainties: the particular branch of mathematics called statistics has been devised to help us deal with these probabilities.

At their best, modern techniques of management, however scientific, are not considered as sources of ready-made answers. They are a means of exploration or a testing apparatus. If we use statistical methods, for instance, we may spark off new thoughts. At the very least we shall have other, rigorously argued, assumptions to put against those of our own prejudices and hunches, those we inherit or which envelop us. Even over-simplification can be a most salutary exercise: it too is a method of confronting our existing practices and assumptions with a stylised version of what analysis suggests is essential to the system. We can illustrate the point by beginning with a very crude model. Since one of our basic problems is that of resources it seems proper that it should come from economics.

Input–output analysis

One of the main determinants of LEA policy at present is budgeting: a rudimentary, and in its traditional form rather unsatisfactory, economic planning technique. The resources required are set out in categories so that education or finance committees, and the like, can see how the money is proposed to be spent. There is, perhaps, a glimmer of the systems approach in this though the image often used

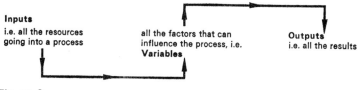

Inputs
i.e. all the resources
going into a process

all the factors that can
influence the process, i.e.
Variables

Outputs
i.e. all the results

Figure 3

to describe it—priming the pump—indicates that the system envisaged is a very simple one. These resources—or inputs—are poured in, and so far as the budget is concerned the results—or outputs— are not considered. (Closer study of the budget will come later. Here the purpose is rather to say a little more about inputs and outputs.)

There is an economic process known as input–output analysis. Its direct relevance to education is problematical but what may be useful to us is the notion of applying a simple pattern to thinking about a complex social service. It is illustrated in Figure 3. In financial terms the process is concerned with predicting not just what will be spent (a self-fulfilling prophecy in the public service) but also how the resources being used will be influenced both by each other and by other factors; and what the outcome will be.

It is, mercifully, no part of my purpose to try to demonstrate the validity of the full rigour of the process when applied even to industry, for which it was designed, let alone to education. It can help, though, by enabling us to look at inputs in a new way, seeing how they relate to each other; by trying to foresee what permutations of circumstance may work on them; and, above all, by considering outputs (i.e. results) not necessarily as direct consequences but as out-turn. As we shall see later, this objective approach—free, for example, of notions of praise or blame, and free from assumption—can be a most useful planning tool.

Cost-benefit analysis

A logical extension of this approach is cost–benefit analysis, which tries to measure, other things being equal, the benefits of a project against its likely cost. Few in education will be able to subdue their scepticism, even if other things were ever equal, about the possibility of quantifying the advantages of an educational scheme. Again one might suggest that the method may be useful even if it does not fulfil exactly what it promises: like most of the techniques discussed here its main function in educational planning should be that of testing assumptions. The process by which cost–benefit analysis can do this is two-fold: first, by winnowing out those processes that are in fact capable of being quantified;* second, even in areas of subjective judgment, by measuring our intuition against a process that seeks to be precise. The process can have the effect of forcing us to consider our basic attitudes.

Think, for instance, of the attempts to measure what education contributes to economic growth. One of the best known is based on the theory that differences in earnings between various sectors of a community reflect the contribution they make to the economy: earnings depend on skill and skill is related to educational achievement. We know that there is a close link between educational background and earnings over a lifetime. So if we regard educational costs as capital investment we can see what the rate of return is: we can find out what increased productivity, measured by increased earnings, comes from higher education and therefore, perhaps, suggest how much we should invest on higher education rather than other forms of capital investment.

There is no need to spend long stating the objections to this. Teachers will not need reminding that some groups, highly educated, make a contribution to social welfare that is not reflected in their earnings. And anyone (particularly with systems theory in mind) can see that there is an array of interrelated factors—environment, opportunity, social class, for example—that affect the situation. In

* If we here consider education in all its aspects we may find there is a surprising amount. The bigger the amount the smaller the area of subjective judgment, which we may agree will be most effective if supported by substantial objective supporting evidence.

any event, is this an adequate view of the value of education? The approach forces us to try to clarify what we think education is in fact for.

The value of confronting vague personal assumptions with rational analysis should not be underestimated even when the analysis is crude and may seem to be wide of the mark. (On what basis is our own estimate of the situation made?) The value of analysis is increased if our judgments are formed, as so often, by reference to the consensus, which may stem from the interplay of many vested interests, prejudice, pressure groups and habit.

Cost–effectiveness analysis

A related, but more flexible, and so for our purposes more useful technique is cost–effectiveness analysis. This is concerned with the relative effectiveness and costs of alternative ways of achieving the same objective: it takes into account benefits other than economic ones. It can work in two directions: given the need to use a particular means of achieving an objective, how can costs be kept to a minimum, or conversely, given a certain amount of money what is the best way of working towards an objective? The process follows a logical sequence, expressed numerically; a model of the various choices is set up, and they are marked according to the way they meet the criterion of (estimated) cost in relation to (estimated) performance.

Again we may often have to be satisfied by the incidental advantages of using the process rather than any convincing answers. For example, if we are to try to relate achievement of objectives to expenditure we need to be fairly specific about our objectives; and we have to try to grade the extent to which they are achieved. This graduation need not necessarily be quantification: expert judgments and the findings of research and past experience can be used with suitable safeguards to test the extent to which they may be valid. Nevertheless, much of the value may lie in the discipline of doing the exercises rather than in finding absolute answers.

The process itself is one that most administrators and policy-makers use intuitively: indeed, the kind of decisions the technique is designed to help us with are those we have to make every day of our lives: such as, at its lowest level, shall I go by bus or take the car? In education we might consider whether to use additional teachers to set up nursery classes or to reduce the size of the teaching group in the infant schools, or whether to raise the school-leaving age. We are in effect saying that, in choosing, we have to trade-off against the benefit we expect to get from one choice the loss of benefit we would have got from one of the other choices; cost–effectiveness analysis seeks to help us measure these relative benefits.

Statistics

The predominance of relative values in education, the acceptance that this must be so, is reflected in the difficulty we have in measurement. It is not merely that examinations—to take a basic example—cannot hope to measure character, moral worth, endeavour and all the other things we set store by; nor is it merely that even the most sophisticated test cannot elucidate the essential appreciation of a subject by a pupil; we find that the very results themselves are no more than relative indications. Physical measurement is simple—there is a zero point on the scale and that represents, in fact, zero. But a score of zero in a geography test means nothing of the kind, but simply that the particular test elicited no response; not that the candidate has no knowledge but rather that he had not enough knowledge to get on to the scale. Educational measurement is therefore relative, not absolute; and statistics, which deals in probabilities, not absolutes, is the mathematical technique best suited to it.

Naturally enough, statistical method, often known as stochastic, is more appropriate to the many aspects of planning in which there is uncertainty than to the deterministic methods of mathematics itself: though strictly mathematical formulae can—and sometimes should—be used as part of the process of providing a firm quantitative basis for value judgments. Both mathematics and statistics are concerned with making inferences as a result of classification and measurement; but statistics tries to do this in the teeth of uncertainty, including of course prediction, which is inference about what will happen in the future.

Educationists have an initial advantage as planners in that many of the basic statistical techniques are the daily currency of schools. The normal curve of distribution, for instance, is a familiar sight in relation to the intelligence quotients of a large group of children, and standard deviation, a fundamental concept, is used to show how individuals perform in relation to others: we know that the distribution of IQs is normal with a mean of 100 and a standard deviation of 15. Educationists readily accept too that IQs are not meaningful in themselves, but depend on how they relate to those of others: they are used in testing by converting actual marks into points on a percentile scale which shows in 100 equal subdivisions how a larger sample of the population than that being tested scored.

Sampling theory is another fundamental statistical technique: for instance it is the basis not only of standardising tests but also of market research. (Although chapter 1 said harsh things about the way this is sometimes used, it has been of enormous influence in our social life, and to criticise its misuse is not to ignore its value.)

Another familiar notion is that of correlation, the extent to which two things, such as sets of marks, are similar to or agree with each other, expressed through a coefficient of correlation ranging in value from +1 (for perfect agreement) to −1 (for complete disagreement). When for example there is a high correlation between the results of two tests, one can predict the results of the second from performance in the first. Correlation is an important tool in prediction which is of the utmost value in planning as well as in teaching. (Any reservations one has about prediction in education are equally applicable to planning: usually what is being predicted is an average which is made up, by definition, of individual variations from it.) Regression analysis enables us to plot curves from observed data and not only to project them into the future but also to calculate the limits within which the forecast might be accurate.

Knowing the limitations of our techniques, this last refinement is of course extremely important. With this it is reasonable to say that even when values, as so often in education, are relative, we still have effective measurement tools. Objective review is not dependent on absolute standards.

Operational research

It is just as well for us that this is so, for a formidable battery of management techniques, operational research (OR), was developed largely out of the demands of the uncertainties of war, notably that of 1939–45. In a war-time situation it was essential for us to try, in order to avoid enormous loss of life and materials, to experiment not through trial and error but in theory, predicting a likely outcome when it was put into practice.

Operational research scientists were able to set up mathematical models (as in a scientific description of the physical world) to represent the elements in the situation and the relationship between them. Their first steps were therefore: setting out the problem logically and constructing mathematical models. In quantifying like this they were clearly ignoring individual variations, using the 'laws' we apply to our world rather like actuarial statistics which predict general life-expectancy but not that of individuals. The mathematics used for the purpose is based on probability theory: a model can be built that produces the same spread as actually occurs by chance. The remaining stages in the process are then: to work out a solution to the problem from the model, test the model and provide controls for the model and then for the reality.

Much of the range of OR concepts has a possible application to the education service. *Inventory*, meaning here 'idle resources', is one. How much stock should be held in reserve, to avoid shortages and production hold-ups, stabilise costs and so on, without tying up too much capital and physical resources? Probability theory can work out an optimum stock level and order policy designed to balance the pros and cons. One obvious application—apart from stock itself—is the training and supply of teachers. *Queueing* problems are a variant: how many staff do you need to avoid either customers or staff being kept waiting? *Allocation* problems can be solved by linear programming, a technique which has been found useful in allocating pupils to secondary schools on the basis of data fed into computers, giving test scores, heads' assessments, lists of possible schools chosen by parents and so on. *Routing* problems, such as the best routes for fleets of school buses, have been tackled by the Local Government Operational Research Unit. *Replacement* problems exist in education as in other industries—furniture, retirement of staff and so on—and the cost–effective policy can be worked out by OR. *Search* techniques were developed to find the best strategy for searching for submarines, and are now being used in accounting: today it is increasingly recognised that management decision-making is frequently not as good as it should be because of insufficient attention to organised searching for alternatives.

There is obviously much to be gained from *sequencing* operations in the most effective way: the building of a new school is a complex project requiring careful planning and scheduling. A number of techniques of network analysis are by now well known: one is critical path method, identifying potential bottlenecks by picking out stages of the operation where there is no margin of time so that they are critical to the exercise; a particular application of it is programme evaluation and review technique (PERT). PERT lays out the network of activities for a project, giving alternative estimates (of time or costs) of the various stages and of the effect one will have on another. Apart from prediction, PERT can show in the early stages of a project what are the prospects of completion on time within cost limits and thus give the planner a chance of doing something about it before it is too late.

No rigidly mathematical models can be devised for these sequencing methods, but with computer simulation of the problem the various combinations can be quickly compared with each other. Computers using these methods have also begun to make themselves useful in doing many of the chores associated with timetabling.

We should say a special word about *competitive problems*, for OR tackles them in a way that is rightly assuming an increasingly important role in management education. Operational gaming is another less rigidly mathematical technique based on simulation. Here the rules of a game (usually a competitive situation) are built into a computer programme, or in simpler games a manual equivalent, for evaluation of the different ploys developed by the teams (perhaps

D

representing firms competing for a share of the market). The simulation technique may be used in other than competitive situations and by now many hundreds of heads of schools will have engaged in 'operation out-basket' or 'candidate selection' simulation exercises. Operational research is not a body of knowledge but an approach to solving problems by trying to categorise, formalise and order its parts and relate them to each other. Its exploration of different types of problem illustrates its open-mindedness, its belief that if we look at the situation from all the angles, a solution will be found. It follows therefore that one of its characteristic features is a grouping together of experts from many different disciplines to see which one, or combination, might be the best. This approach seems to have a particular potential for the education service, which embraces all disciplines and skills, and in which team-teaching is increasingly widely used to ensure that these are all fully employed.

Management information systems

It is one of our hoarier platitudes that any decision is only as good as the information on which it is based. We have discussed earlier the key position of information in any open system, and its ambiguous status on account of its ability to shape the system it enters. Here we are concerned with the technique of using it. The principle that applies is just as platitudinous—the more complicated the system, the better organised its information system needs to be.

A management information system has three basic functions: collection, processing and distribution of data. In the education service it should ideally weld together data for the instructional and the administrative parts of the enterprise, including any mechanical or electronic aids. In how many educational units—schools, colleges, education offices or government departments—does this happen? Even at the level of record-keeping we are likely to have a very mixed bag: some duplication; certain periods when life seems to consist of nothing but filling up forms; an *ad hoc* assemblage of materials and procedures.

And a management information system is more than records: it is the life line of any organisation. As with the other techniques we have discussed it can be studied and implemented at a very sophisticated level: here we are concerned to sketch out a crude version to illustrate the possibilities. In essence our minimum requirement should be that our flow of data should be so ordered that it helps systematic planning and ensures that related data-collection -processing and -distribution activities are aware of each other's existence.

First, data *collection*. We may begin by categorising our needs. Let us start by identifying six types of information requirement: for

(a) pupils, (b) curriculum, (c) personnel, (d) physical resources, (e) financial and (f) administration: and subdividing each for (i) internally required and (ii) externally required information. We may then list all the types of records we keep, forms we fill in, and so on: for example, student record cards, medical cards, annual revenue estimate return, staffing returns, requisitions, timetables, reports for committees. We can then set them out according to categories, perhaps according to a pattern like this:

Pupils   (a) individual records: academic
          (b) individual records: other
          (c) numbers projection

Curriculum   (a) curriculum-planning
             (b) timetabling

Personnel   (a) personal documentation, salaries, etc.
            (b) numbers projections, schemes of allowance, etc.
            (c) in-service training

Physical resources   (a) buildings
                     (b) equipment
                     (c) books, stationery and materials
                     (d) transport
                     (e) catering

Financial   (a) revenue budget
            (b) accounts

Administration   (a) regulations
                 (b) committee reports

From this we should be able to prepare a chart showing what overlaps there might be—in a school, for example, between records required by the office and those needed internally; in an education office between those used for the committee's annual report and those wanted by the DES—or small differences in design that might enable one return to replace two. We can take the opportunity to consider whether all are needed (some are hallowed only by time) and to look carefully at how well those that are required fulfil their purpose. Some gaps may become evident, too. Eventually a definitive list will appear. If we next plot a time-scale indicating when each of these is needed throughout the year, we have the beginnings of an ordered management information system.

Data-*processing* is increasingly being carried out today by computers; and universities, polytechnics and education authorities are finding new uses for them in education management information systems. However, it would be quite wrong to suggest that such systems are dependent on electronic operation. For one thing, as well as questions of cost there are ethical considerations: the idea of a data bank from which information can be drawn like water from a tap is attractive, but it may have dangerous implications for the invasion of privacy. Suitability for computer-processing needs to be thought out carefully. In any case, no computer can design the process: a good deal of initial systems analysis is needed first. This means thinking about needs and setting them down in an orderly fashion: a system designed for manual operation is, in most circumstances, a sensible preliminary to going over to computer use. The collection of data and its distribution, the other essential parts of an information system, have also to be arranged. So for most of us the most important requirement is not access to a computer but a systematic survey of needs on a common-sense basis, and an equally common-sense implementation of the system.

From theory to practice

Techniques enable theories to be put into practice. This brief survey did not set out to explore fully the subtleties of the various examples chosen, but rather to look at a range of techniques as indicators of a style of thought, a cast of mind. Apart from indicating their intrinsic value in relation to specific problems, presenting them in this way may help to show them as facets of a whole and thus as appropriate instruments for applying aspects of systems theory to educational planning. This application is the theme of the remaining chapters.

5 Planning and estimates

If we conducted an opinion survey throughout the education service asking the crude question: 'Which do we need most: more money, or better planning?', we would perhaps find very few enthusiasts for planning. No amount of planning can make up for inadequate resources, of course, but good plans take into account what is likely to be available and use it to the best advantage: allocation of resources is an essential part of planning. And the best plans strengthen arguments for more resources.

Yet for most of us in the education service, planning and finance are two separate exercises. We may be asked to share in making decisions about educational policy, great or small. We may be asked to state our financial requirements (though our share in decision-making here is likely to be less). The two processes are usually quite separate.

The annual budget

For most of us the moment of truth comes each year with the compilation, scrutiny and eventual approval of the annual revenue estimates. All our proposals stand or fall by this exercise. It is of crucial importance for our plans but as a planning tool it falls far short of what is needed.

In the first place, the form in which the estimates are required by treasurers on behalf of councils and their finance and education committees is related more to control of expenditure, to accounting for it, than to planning its outlay. Its structure is usually concerned with categories of expenditure—e.g. teaching-staff salaries, superannuation, caretakers' wages, repairs and maintenance, books, stationery and materials—rather than with estimating the cost of particular projects—e.g. converting secondary grammar and modern schools to comprehensive, setting up a remedial teaching service. This exercise, if it is done at all, takes place separately from the budgeting process.

However, an education budget will usually be subdivided into expenditure on, say, primary, secondary and further education. This means that the projected cost of teachers' salaries will be set out in three or four separate blocks according to the branch of the service concerned, and submitted to the appropriate subcommittee of the education committee. To this extent the costing is applied to broad programmes, i.e. the work of a subcommittee. For planning purposes, though, this is too crude a format: the activities lying behind the different subheadings—teaching, caretaking, supplying materials, etc.—are different in kind; some may be ancillary to others and so on. The true costs of the various parts of the service are likely to be concealed in any event by such devices as the sharing of costs of central administrative charges, such as architect's, treasurer's or clerk's department costs, on a notional basis, by the conversion of certain capital costs (of buildings or equipment) on the revenue account, and so on.

It is rare in local government for the different departments to be allowed to devise their own pattern of estimating expenditure: the treasurer naturally prefers a standard format. (He prefers, too, the estimate pattern to match that in which he keeps his accounts.) And treasurers nationally, in order to be able to compare each other's costs, have agreed on a standard form of account. The result, in terms of estimates as a planning tool, is unfortunate: the tail (accounts) wags the dog (estimates). Estimating by adding a certain amount to last year's total is encouraged by this stylisation in which the relationship of costs to activities is obscured.

Then again, when the form of the estimates becomes stereotyped, initiative is stifled and the particular requirements of different areas and different services tend to be concealed. One particular complication for education services relates to the difference between the budget year, usually 1 April to 31 March, and the academic year, say 1 September to 31 August. This means, for example, that costs of salaries of additional teachers (the bulk of whom start in September) are represented by only seven-twelfths of what their salaries will cost in a full year. It also means that an extra five-twelfths of the previous year's additional amount is committed for the next budget. So that even 'last year plus 10 per cent' may well not represent 10 per cent of new activities, increased salaries or other improvements: some of it is likely to be hang-overs from the past.

Such a short time-span is inadequate for planning purposes: it would obviously be better to look further ahead. In practice we tend to look further back—to the last completed financial year to see how it turned out. To do this in the same short space of time as reviewing the progress of spending in the current year and forming estimates for next, places undue emphasis on the technical aspects of the exercise and not enough on evaluation.

What goes into the system and what it costs tend to be given more attention than what comes out at the other end. With such a time-scale the costing of inputs is the major part of the exercise: salary costs, number of teachers, rates, heat, light and water costs—these are the basic stuff of the estimates. Additional staff or equipment arising from committee resolutions, proposals stemming from consultations with teachers, and projects arising from pressure by individual administrators, heads of schools or advisers, are assembled, costed and included or excluded 'on merit'. (Committee resolutions are included *ex officio*, as it were, and the rest are measured by a variety of standards—cherished items, e.g. for extra allowances for teachers or additional laboratory stewards, may be submitted year after year and eventually slip through as a result of a process of attrition.)

All the examples, it should be noted, relate to specific items (such as staff) rather than to programmes (such as introducing metrication or raising the school-leaving age). This is typical of the pattern. It helps to explain why, with so much concern for inputs, little attention may be given to 'outputs', the educational impact of what is provided. It is assumed that the items will achieve their (assumed) objective.

Nor is the pattern helpful in considering priorities. When it comes to fixing what goes in the estimate or, later, what should be cut out, there is an order of precedence, either explicit or implicit, something like this:

1 inescapable commitments: e.g. salaries of existing staff; rent and rates; central administration charges;
2 virtually inescapable commitments: e.g. staff salaries for the second year of new further education courses started the previous year; extra costs of new schools it is planned to open;
3 necessary provision but where there is some discretion as to the actual amount to be set aside; e.g. repairs and maintenance; books, stationery, materials and equipment; awards to students;
4 discretionary matters:
   (a) new ventures already approved by the education committee;
   (b) other proposals.

True, these are the realities of the situation: no point in including large sums for new ventures if you put nothing in for what you have to pay. But this is not the complete story. The built-in assumption that nothing in the 4(b) category can be contemplated until all the other categories are taken care of may sometimes mean that radical alternatives are not being considered. Habitual spending, which may not get results, is encouraged.

Of course, experienced educators, administrators and committees do consider alternatives and sometimes radical ones. The point is that the budget may discourage their doing so. In practice such revaluations either happen *ad hoc* or intuitively or, if formally, then at some other time (and by other people) than the estimates. Yet estimates time is when it matters, when the options are still open.

The two main weaknesses of traditional budgeting seem to be, then:

(i) failure to relate costs to educational impact, and
(ii) separation of estimating from policy-making.

Output budgeting

In recent years attempts have been made to grapple with these problems. Education Planning Paper No. 1 (1970), *Output Budgeting for the Department of Education and Science*, describes one of them.

Traditionally, budgets have categorised expenditure by the type of resource on which it is to be spent—staff, buildings, materials and so on—rather than by the purpose for which it is to be spent. The aims of an output budgeting system may briefly be stated as being to analyse expenditure by the purpose for which it is to be spent and to relate it to the results achieved. It is a formal system for establishing:

(i) what a department is aiming to achieve—what its *objectives* are—in the areas of policy for which it is responsible;
(ii) which *activities* are contributing to these objectives;
(iii) what resources, or *inputs*, are being devoted to these activities;
(iv) what is actually being achieved, or what the *outputs* are.

As the authors of the paper say, 'Output budgeting has to be considered as a system, and not just as a new way of setting out . . . tables of figures'. They suggest that the name used in Canada and the USA, 'planning–programming–budgeting system' (PPBS), better indicates what it is all about. Their introduction implies that had the report been written in 1970 (and not completed by January 1969), this is the term they would have used.

Their reasons—that PPBS can in fact be used where measurement and costing of outputs is particularly difficult (as in education), and that it better conveys the linking of planning and budgeting—are valid. There is another reason. Approaching the problem as an attempt to improve budgeting methods may conceal the fact that there are very many weaknesses in our planning processes quite apart from those associated with the traditional budgeting pattern.

Policy-making in education tends to be based on untested value judgments. The difficulties of testing these judgments are well known and the reader will not need to be reminded of them. Most of us put up with the situation reluctantly, telling ourselves that time will in the end tell. Unfortunately, the more organised the provision of education becomes the less chance there is of the results of bad judgments becoming apparent. Educational planning is in the nature of a self-fulfilling prophecy. Perhaps the best example is that of educational subnormality. The 1944 Education Act provides for referral of children suspected of incapacity to learn to a medical officer, implying that educational subnormality is a medical condition and that objective standards can be applied to it; and in practice educational subnormality has come to be equated with 'ascertainment' in relation to admission to special schools. The result is that an authority with a large proportion of places in these schools ascertains a higher percentage of its pupils than an authority with a smaller proportion. To some extent, places are provided according to estimated need but all building policy, which may be based on principle, hunch, shortage of money or availability of land, has an arbitrary element. The element of self-fulfilling prophecy about this is that once assigned to such a school a child is likely to conform to the expectation implied in its ascertainment.

The human capacity for rationalisation, in the Freudian sense, is infinite, so that people are usually happy to build a superstructure of logic on top of assumptions. The internal logic of the process is unshakable but it may be based on false premises, and the problem in education is that there are no absolute standards by which premises can be tested. In Britain we cannot escape this dilemma by government edicts expressing inflexible tenets as in a totalitarian society. Nor, because of our pride in being practical, do we put much trust in attempts to test our assumptions by abstract thought. We rely largely on the consensus and the apparatus of partnership that seeks to determine it and implement its findings. We concentrate on means rather than ends and we often confuse the two.

Thus one of our favourite slogans today relates to equality of opportunity. To some extent the wide acceptance of this concept reflects the broad measure of agreement on social policy by all but the most extreme. But that it also reflects failure to think through its implications is clear whenever someone tries to put it into practice: there is violent disagreement about what constitutes equal opportunity. This, surely, is the point at which questions should be asked about what the equality of opportunity is for: what are the ends to which this is the means? When these questions are asked we come up against the real disagreements: on whether economic prosperity is our goal (and if so how best to help this educationally) or whether the prosperity is itself a means to an end; on what this end really is.

Management by objectives

Small wonder, then, that management by objectives has as yet made little inroad into the practices of the education service. To the self-fulfilling prophecy we must, in education, add the public service tradition. Dickens invented a Circumlocution Department, peopled with Barnacles, who when challenged in Parliament as being 'abominable and Bedlamite', responded by recounting how many thousands of letters and memoranda had been written and how many miles of stationery had been consumed in the process. The great bulk of those who work in most organisations are far removed from the policy-making front: they work on tram-lines laid down from above. So policies and purposes change but processes continue willy-nilly, and bureaucrats confuse producing memoranda with achieving objectives.

Producing a memorandum, like teaching a class, is a task not an objective. Most people, asked why they are employed in such-and-such a place, will reply in terms of the tasks they perform, not of what they are trying to achieve. The reader may like to try one or other small experiment to test this out: he can look at the job description of the post he now holds, if there is one; or the last one he received (or produced) as further particulars for an advertised post; or put his head out of his office and ask the first person he sees. He will be a rare exception if he discovers reference to objectives rather than tasks or duties. Senior managers concerned about inefficiency or poor performance tend to look towards the organisation, to create new posts or redistribute duties. Education officers are often preoccupied with institutional management. School hours and holidays make more sense as arrangements convenient to teachers than as a framework to teaching children.

Considering objectives implies looking further than one's nose-end. Not just 'to teach' or even 'to teach children to read by the time they are six'—though that is a vast improvement—but to do so for a stated purpose. We shall be dealing in more detail in later chapters with ways of identifying objectives: at this stage I am merely concerned to emphasise the need to make the attempt, a need rarely fulfilled in the public services or in educational establishments.

This is not, of course, merely an aberration of the public services. There are plenty of recorded instances in industry of unreflecting perpetration of processes that have long since lost their point.

Management by objectives is in some ways more an attitude of mind than a technique, and it would be ludicrous if an approach dedicated to keeping managerial eyes focused on ends rather than means were to emphasise unduly the means by which this end should be achieved. However, in order to stress that attitudes can be most effective when supported systematically, it may be helpful to indicate the stages in a typical management-by-objectives exercise. First, establish long-range-objectives for the organisation. Second, see that the organisation is structurally capable of carrying them out. Third, derive functional objectives for the various branches, with the emphasis on results rather than tasks. Fourth, explain the objectives to key subordinates and encourage them to follow the same process. Fifth, ensure that specific goals are established and agreed by managers and subordinates. Sixth, map out a course of action for achieving these goals. Seventh, establish systematic reviews of progress and feedback of information. Once this stage is reached the process begins again: it is a cycle rather than a once-for-all-exercise.

Even in industry, setting targets for management may be an accidental and *ad hoc* process applied to parts of an organisation in response to specific needs, rather than the result of organised planned effort on the lines described above. The concept and its implications for the communication of information were still sufficiently novel to be described* in the mid-1960s as a 'new approach'.

But it is worse in public authorities. For one thing, the fairly clear-cut indicators of quantitative success or failure in industry encourage regular revaluation. For another, there may well be fewer processes in industry designed apparently to uphold moral standards rather than to achieve objectives efficiently. Financial procedures in local government, for instance, often appear to be largely concerned with preventing people from running away to South America with the proceeds. Naturally this is important and the fact that the procedures by themselves would be ludicrously inadequate to prevent such adventures is beside the point. The tradition this embodies extends far beyond preserving the integrity of officials; into, for example, the system of checking accounts sent in by outside firms for payment. No efficient business firm would spend annually ten times as much on checking these as is ever recovered from the discovery of errors.

So far as education authorities are concerned, administrators and teachers and, in their different way, elected members are frequently confronted by vast issues of principle, stupendous questions of theory. They have philosophies and can often articulate them. But philosophies are not objectives; nor is there much indication of large-scale movement towards running authorities or schools on the lines of management by objectives. In the official process of administering the service such consideration of objectives as there is tends to be conducted separately from the budgeting process by which resources are allocated.

* By Dale and Michelon in *Modern Management Methods*, Cleveland: World Publishing Company, 1966; Harmondsworth: Penguin, 1969.

Planning–programming–budgeting system

The method known as a planning–programming–budgeting system
seeks not only to associate the two processes but to initiate thinking
about fundamentals. It includes:

1 review of the programmes being undertaken, including: (a)
   testing ʼthe validity of the stated or implied objectives (the
   ends), and (b) alternative methods of achieving them (the
   means);
2 setting up performance measures and ways of costing the educational impact of what is being done.

Though American in its present form, PPBS owes something at
least to English thought—the stimulus given by J. M. Keynes to
the notion of the planned economy and in particular its influence on
President F. D. Roosevelt in introducing the New Deal in the 1930s.
We in Britain have been in daily contact with the political applications of such thinking and have seen in the various upheavals in
the Civil Service—the changing departmental structures, the setting
up of counterweights to the Treasury, the decline in importance of
the Chancellor's annual performance—manifestations of the dissatisfaction felt with traditional budgeting.

As early as 1949 in the USA, the Hoover Commission recommended
'performance budgeting' for the federal government. This was developed most extensively in the Department of Defense which
introduced 'program budgeting' in 1961. In crude terms, the previous
system could tell you the cost of all the army equipment but not the
cost of waging a war. Planning and budgeting began to be by 'missions'
rather than categories: the use of this kind of terminology has
served to produce some rather bewildering jargon, but the metaphor
itself is perhaps not a bad one for those engaged in fighting wars
against ignorance and deprivation.

By now in Canada and the USA, submissions are made according
to programmes by all spending departments to the appropriate
Treasury department. In this country less dramatic changes have
been made. Our set of initials, PESC, refers to the Public Expenditure
Survey Committee, which has some features of programme budgeting, notably looking at expenditure in 'functional blocks' rather
than by departments, and taking a five-year span. However, functions
are not the same as objectives, so that the link between policy-
making and costing is not fully made. Much of the credit for developing the PPBS notion goes to an American research and development (RAND) organisation. The RAND Corporation in the 1950s
sponsored research which revealed the wider possibilities of the

PPBS and refined it to a stage where it has become a practical proposition.

On this side of the Atlantic the method is less well known. It is advocated by one of the best known of the management consultants that local authorities are now beginning to employ, but probably most people in education learned it first from the DES Planning Paper. If they did they were perhaps not entirely convinced of its value. As a comment in *Higher Education Review* said: '. . . a document proposing a completely different approach to planning and control of expenditure ought to have had more impact.'

The reason it did not, according to the *Review*, is not far to seek. 'The difficulty is in the approach itself.' The comments in this article—which are entirely fair—no doubt reflect the views of many readers of the Planning Paper. After pointing out a number of snags the *Review* concedes some possibilities (such as: 'At the very least it will make people think about what they are doing . . .', and: 'any system that assists government to consider what its objectives in any policy are, what activities contribute to them and what are the financial and other implications of a policy, must be almost wholly good'.) But its final sentence reflects the whole tone of the piece: 'Provided we can find out *how* to do it.'

The method seems to me to have so many possibilities as to make it worth the effort to find out how. It is undeniable that applying it to education poses special problems: the task of fixing objectives, performance measures and standards of evaluation is a difficult one. But if it is accepted that PPBS, like all good management techniques, is of more value in posing relevant questions than in providing ready-made answers, it may not seem quite so formidable.

So in outlining in the remaining chapters the process as it might be applied to education, the aim will be to stimulate thought and to suggest the potentiality of the method rather than to present a ready-made planners' charter. To say that it exemplifies the systems approach and that fully developed it is a total system is not to suggest that it is likely to be totally satisfactory nor that it can only be applied by an enormous outlay of labour and resources to a whole education authority service or to the DES. If its aims are taken to be considerably more modest—stimulating constructive thinking—and its range of application is taken to include small segments of the education service, then, paradoxically, the value is likely to be very much greater.

Although the origin of PPBS may be in dissatisfaction with conventional budgeting, the budget it produces is not the whole, nor even the main part, of its function. Quite apart from its long-term potential as an integrating force leading towards a complete systems approach, we can point to the possibility that it may satisfy three basic requirements in education, requirements that may otherwise often conflict with each other:

1   relevance to the needs of pupils and students and the community generally;
2   democratic decision-making; and
3   value for money.

The first of these—relevance—is kept to the fore by the alignment of PPBS towards objectives. This also helps the second—democracy—for greater attention to ends rather than means makes easier, and makes more desirable, the involvement of elected members, teachers and the public, since it puts technical skill in its proper place. The third—value for money—arises not simply from measuring costs but from weighing the success of existing policies in achieving agreed objectives and adjusting them accordingly.

The application of PPBS is presented here, then, not as a new and esoteric technique but as the use of ordered common sense. It is a game that anyone can play. In the next chapter we shall skim quickly through the rules before beginning more detailed study.

6 The mechanics of PPBS

Planning, to be meaningful, has to be more than just devising schemes. It must include, as a minimum:

1 formulating and analysing objectives;
2 assessing resources; and
3 preparing phased programmes designed to achieve the objectives effectively and economically.

PPBS is a method of doing this as a process rather than *ad hoc* and in separate stages. Its assumption is that in order to allocate resources meaningfully it is necessary to analyse and review the whole system.

In this chapter the aim is to give an outline of the procedure before going into details of each part of it later. So as not to lose track, few examples will be given: the pattern is what is being demonstrated. This pattern can be applied at any level, from ministry to school, but for simplicity the level assumed here is that of the LEA, and the responsibility for initiating the technical side of the exercise is taken to be that of the education officer. (He will obviously need the co-operation of the treasurer to carry out the exercise, and the agreement of the council to implement it.)

Philosophy

The first concern is to establish the *philosophy* of our organisation (or institution, venture or whatever). For an LEA we might find the raw material for our investigation of this in committee resolutions, government or council policy statements, reports from advisory committees, and of course through consultation with teachers' associations, parents, students and the public at large.

Thus even at this stage democratic participation can be ensured. Consultation is always more meaningful when it is for a specific purpose, something more than keeping 'the other side' in the picture. Here its aim can be very specific. Part of establishing a philosophy in a democracy is *identifying needs*, and this is related to (though not identical with) discovering wants. The more trouble taken over this the better the whole exercise is likely to be done.

Figure 4 shows some of the possible stages in the operation of identifying needs and recording the philosophy of an education authority.

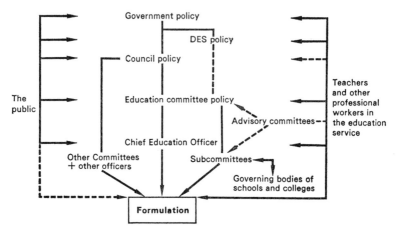

Figure 4 Identifying needs and formulating philosophy

Objectives

A disembodied philosophy is no use to anyone, so next we must consider the implications of the ethos we have sketched out. What kind of things would embody this philosophy? How can we live by it? What *objectives* have we? How do they look when they are written down?

We are still at this stage concerned with ends, not means: we should be thinking for instance of 'educating children under the age of twelve' rather than 'providing primary schools'. (Again this questioning of assumptions may be a valuable exercise in itself, for assumptions are great enemies of progress.)

Programme structures

But ends need means; we have to translate objectives into *programmes*. For this we have to relate what is being done to what we are trying to achieve.

The first stage is recording our current activities. As a beginning a simple stream-of-consciousness technique may be best, writing them down in any order as they come to mind. But, of course, here is another opportunity for debate and discussion with colleagues and anyone else concerned.

A formidable list will begin to grow and it may soon be desirable to subdivide both the list and the task of compiling it. Obvious subdivisions for an LEA would be primary education, secondary education, further education: they can be called *programme categories*. Within the primary sector, pre-school, infant and junior subsections may be chosen, and so on: these subdivisions can be called *programme elements*. The pattern as a whole is called a *programme structure*.

So, depending on the scope of the enterprise, we should soon have a list of programme categories, each matched by a broad objective. Each category will then be subdivided into elements, matched by more specific objectives and a list of the activities we carry out at present in pursuit of these objectives.

Assessment of performance and/or impact

We now have to see how far what we are doing in fact leads towards these objectives; we want to do so in a way that will help us to calculate the costs of our activities and to compare alternative methods from the point of view of likely effectiveness and costs.

We must assess our current *performance* by whatever *measures* we can find and agree upon. The process can be set out as follows:

1 standards required;
2 application of the standard to the actual situation;
3 whether above $(+)$ or below $(-)$ standard and by how much ($\%$).

Use of the word 'performance' suggests that what we are measuring is the efforts of those involved, i.e. whether they are doing their best. To some extent this may be so, but we are also concerned with how effective they are. The *impact* of certain activities may be small even though the performance of those implementing them is high. (For example, a performance measure for an education welfare officer might be the percentage of children attending school; but effectiveness, or impact, would also include consideration of reasons for absence in some areas or for some children and what was being done about them.) We should bear in mind, then, that we need to measure impact here if at all possible.

Assessment of resources

An integral part of measuring impact is assessing the resources expended in achieving whatever results we get. And, at the same time, to build up a total picture of resources required we have to look at

E

whether there is a shortage or whether there is surplus capacity in relation to the specific activities we have listed. The pattern might be:

1   standards (of staffing etc.) achieved;
2   standards required;
3   deficits and surpluses.

Programme budget

In this part of the exercise we have the beginnings of a *programme budget*, a budget pattern in which needs and costs can be related to specific objectives. However, at this stage it can only be a rough indication of what might eventually emerge, for making the objectives specific and translating them into goals is not easy: there are likely to be many different ways of achieving them.

Analysis of issues and alternative approaches

Right from the outset many *issues* will be raised: e.g. whether to adopt the principle of compensatory education, giving extra assistance at school to those in social need. Their *analysis* (and if possible resolution) is an integral part of the system, calling for ordered evaluation of alternative philosophies—and incidentally offering yet another opportunity for democratic involvement. Similarly there will be many occasions when alternative approaches are possible, e.g. whether to set up nursery schools or nursery classes, and these need to be weighed and costed.

Refining of objectives

Throughout the exercise, analysis of implications often shows a need to be more specific about objectives, to refine or even to revise them.

Revision of programme structure

Frequently, too, this analysis casts doubt on the adequacy of the programme structure chosen. As we shall see, there may be many equally valid programme structures for the various aspects of the work. The structure is only a set of pegs on which the analysis is hung and it often matters little which one is chosen. Certainly a good deal of time can be wasted trying to achieve perfection at the beginning of the process: better to settle for something rough and ready and refine it later.

Later revision is usually necessary, particularly if different groups have been working on different programme categories, and decisions will need to be made about where to include the many elements that overlap each other.

Action programmes

The revised programme structure can then be extended to produce *action programmes* with *costs*.

Fixing time-scale and priorities

Normally a period of time is specified for the PPBS. Five years is the one usually chosen, one suspects in deference to the famous Soviet Russian concept of the *pyati-lyetnaya* plan. In fact, for most of us five years is on the long side to be really effective in the later stages. However, substantially more than one year is needed and if the period is considered not so much a forecast relating to specific years as an exercise in establishing priorities, then it can be most useful. As a practical method of translating the conventional annual budget into a costed policy document it is invaluable: the compulsory determination of priorities at estimates time each year is extended over a five-year period and is related to objectives not formal groupings.

Annual programmes and review of process

After this a more detailed programme for the first year is compiled from the five-year one. Once this is approved the cycle begins again: the original five-year period loses its first year and is extended for another year into the future. The whole process is carried through as before until another single year budget can be spun off, and so on. Figure 5 gives an idea of the various stages in the process as they relate to each other.

Figure 6 indicates the time-scale of a PPBS exercise as it might fit into a local education authority pattern. It might, of course, be necessary to have one or more annual trial runs before bringing in the system as a formal management tool.

Organisation

Finally it should be noted that working through this process may well show up certain weaknesses in organisation. Theoretically, if the process is done properly the organisation required should be obvious: a ready-made system should drop out at the end of the production line. Things are unlikely to work out just like that

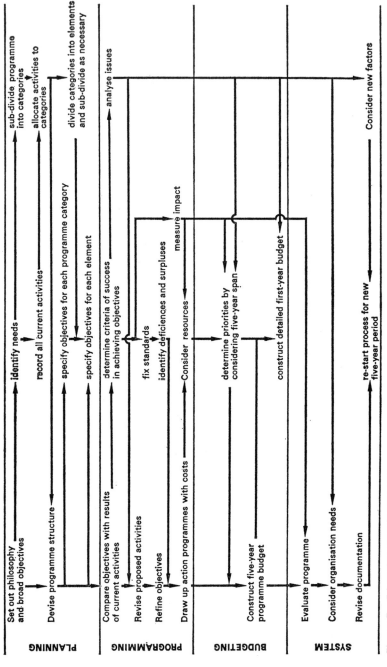

Figure 5   Education programme area

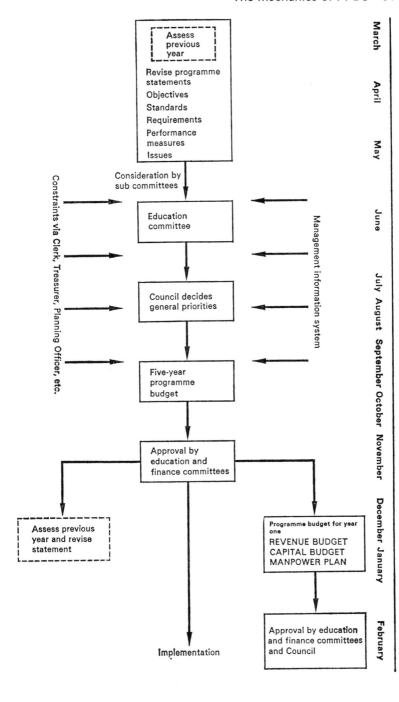

Figure 6 Planning–programming–budgeting cycle in local education authority

but—as with much else in PPBS—there is value in making the attempt. Too often we begin to consider problems by looking at organisation. The simple message of PPBS is to look first to objectives, then try to order the resources to do the job required. It sounds obvious, but it is rarely done that way.

7 Programme statements:
(I) The programme structure

Let us assume that there have been a number of sessions, in the education office, in schools and colleges, in committee rooms or in public at which general philosophy has been discussed and a start has been made at identifying needs. These sessions, if they achieve nothing else, will have the effect of alerting those who may be affected to what is going on. In fact, the sessions should also ensure co-operation and it will be very surprising if they do not produce some bright ideas.

We can then begin compiling a *programme statement*, for the purpose of defining the scope of the programmes we propose to plan. This will include a number of documents:

1 the programme structure;
2 a statement of objectives;
3 a statement of standards required and an application of these standards to the clientele for whom we are catering so as to identify precise needs;
4 a statement of any gaps or surpluses in provision; and
5 an analysis of performance so far in achieving these objectives.

Each of these will be considered in detail in succeeding chapters: we begin here with programme structure.

The whole of the education service is our programme area; but we are in fact dealing with a range of separate if related *programme categories* (such as primary education and secondary education), each of which may be subdivided into *elements* (such as teaching, accommodation, supplies, etc.). We need to state first of all what these categories and elements are and how they relate to each other, to arrange them to form a *programme structure*.

Programme categories

We are looking then for the major activities undertaken by the education service. This particular stage in the exercise, at least, need hold no terrors. Indeed, the biggest danger is that educationists may look for complications that do not exist. Having listened to, and no doubt agreed with, severe criticism of the conventional budget categories as management tools, they may expect to have to scrap everything they have been used to. It is doubtful if they need, for the conventional subdivisions of the education budget in most

63

instances are a logical starting-point for the programme structure. They tend to follow the pattern of the education committee's subcommittees, for whom of course the subdivisions of the budget are normally prepared. There is much to be said for retaining this arrangement as the subcommittees are the natural planning units for the range of work for which they are responsible.

The structure may benefit from modification, however, particularly if some of the subcommittees are responsible for a wide range of work. For example, a schools subcommittee may cover nursery, primary and secondary education, or a further education subcommittee may deal with the youth service and adult education as well as technical colleges and colleges of further education. These not very closely related matters will probably need to be put into programme categories of their own.

Another danger to be avoided if the subcommittee pattern is followed is that of concentrating too much on institutions. A programme is not a collection of institutions; though the institutions may be the main means of achieving the programme's objectives. The very name of a *schools* subcommittee or a *schools* branch of the office may give a misleading slant to the exercise right at the start. A programme category defines a type of activity, not an institution.

Table 1 shows how programme categories were devised from the main activities of an education committee's subcommittees. (A fourth subcommittee, concerned with sites and buildings matters was given

Table 1   **Local education authority programme**

Subcommittees	Main responsibilities	Programme categories
1 Schools	(a) nursery schools	1 Pre-school education
	(b) junior and infant schools	2 Primary education
	(c) secondary schools	3 Secondary education
	(d) school meals and milk	4 Meals and milk
2 Personal services	(a) special schools	5 Education of children with special needs
	(b) school health	
	(c) school attendance and welfare	
3 (i) Further education	(a) colleges of further education	6 Further education
	(b) colleges of education	
	(c) awards	
	(d) youth and community service	7 Recreational, social and cultural education
	(e) evening institutes	
(ii) Youth employment	(f) youth employment service	8 Youth employment

no programme categories of its own: its functions were servicing rather than initiating developments. So the costs of its activities, notably the capital building programme, were allocated for this exercise to the other subcommittees. A fifth, the finance subcommittee was given responsibility for co-ordinating the planning exercise and for advising the education committee on priorities.)

These subdivisions are of course entirely a matter of convenience: they can be altered to suit particular circumstances. They need to represent substantial, yet not too widely ranging blocks of activity. It is usually a good idea, if staffing resources allow it, to set up a small group to work on each category, ideally on operational research lines with a variety of skills looking at the problems. If this is the pattern, however, there should be cross-membership of some of the groups for it will be found that certain activities are shared (or fought over) by more than one group. There should also be an overall co-ordinator, or at least a common convenor ensuring that left hands know what right hands are doing.

Programme elements

The first task of these groups will not be quite so easy as defining the programme categories. Each category needs to be subdivided again into elements (and if necessary into sub-elements): the eight categories listed on pp. 66–7 contain many heterogeneous elements, and these need to be identified, partly to clarify precisely what is done and partly to enable the objectives of the service to be worked out in as meaningful and as specific a way as possible.

It is important to bear in mind from the start that there is not normally one unquestionably right subdivision into elements: a variety of approaches is possible and they may all be right. The aim is to produce a structure that seems to present the programme category in the most logical fashion so that eventually alternative ways of achieving objectives can be considered.

This makes it fairly obvious that the conventional line-by-line subdivisions of the revenue estimates will not be appropriate. Salaries and wages; national insurance; rents and rates; books, stationery and materials: these are in no sense activities designed to achieve educational objectives, and no amount of rearrangement can make them so. Amongst the many possible types of subdivision that we might use it may be helpful to consider two: the client-centred and the activity-centred.

In the first the key is to think of the people for whom the service is intended. In primary education for example, we could subdivide into infant and junior; and perhaps again into areas served by groups of schools, to try to identify children whose social background might require a different approach. Or in the *children with special needs* programme category mentioned above we might subdivide into: children with learning difficulties; children with physical handicap; children with emotional problems; socially disadvantaged children, and so on.

In the second type of subdivision the basis is the different kinds of activity involved in the programme: for example, teaching; supporting teachers by ancillary activites including administration; building schools; transporting children to school.

The examples given below include subdivisions according to both methods.

Programme categories	Elements
1 Pre-school education	(a) Nursery schools
	(b) Nursery classes
	(c) Aids to voluntary activities
2 Primary education	(a) Accommodation
	(b) Teaching
	(c) Support for teaching
	(d) Buildings and grounds
	(e) Services for pupils
	(f) Outside activities
	(g) School management and administration
3 Secondary education	(a) Accommodation
	(b) Teaching
	(c) Support for teaching
	(d) Buildings and grounds
	(e) Services for pupils
	(f) Outside activities
	(g) School government and administration
4 Children with special needs	(a) Children with learning difficulties
	(b) Children with emotional and behavioural difficulties
	(c) Children with physical difficulties
	(d) Socially deprived children
5 Meals and milk	(a) Provision of school meals
	(b) Facilities for production and consumption
	(c) Staffing
	(d) Transport
	(e) Provision of milk
	(f) Further education meals
6 Further education	(a) Teacher training
	(b) Higher and advanced further education
	(c) Non-advanced further education

7 Social, cultural and recreational education	(a) Youth service
	(b) Community service
	(c) Formal adult education
8 Youth employment service	(a) Careers information and advice
	(b) Employment
	(c) Agency services
	(d) Special needs

The best kind of structure will emerge as a result of discussion and a good deal of trial and error. No doubt as the method is more widely used, standard programme elements may be devised that can be used everywhere. There would be advantages in this, but a good deal would be lost if they were applied unreflectingly, for much of the value is in working out how the various strands of the service fit together.

It is quite usual in practice for working groups engaged on a PPBS exercise to start off with one pattern and to change it part-way through the exercise. Any formation can only be an approximation and only trial and error and practice will show which is the right one for the particular circumstances.

Programme sub-elements

In any event we have to subdivide the elements still further if we are to identify meaningful objectives: the more precise they are the more useful they become. The elements listed above are inadequate in a number of ways. For example, the pre-school education category includes an element 'aids to voluntary activities' intended to cover grants to playgroups and private nurseries. The element might well need to be subdivided accordingly to help in defining policies which might be different in relation to the different kinds of voluntary activity.

The example on p. 66 shows up a weakness of the primary, secondary and further education programmes. As set out there they seem to cover only direct provision by the education authority, whereas of course at all three stages education authorities assist their own residents who go to institutions provided by other bodies. A primary school child whose parents move just beyond the boundaries of a town may still be allowed to continue as an extra-district pupil at his former school. Or a secondary school pupil may go to a direct grant school or an independent boarding school. And many thousands of university and further education students receive grants to go to institutions all over the country and even abroad.

We can overcome this problem thus:

Programme categories
Primary education

Elements	Sub-elements
A Maintaining schools	(a) Accommodation (b) Teaching (c) Support for teaching (d) Building and grounds (e) Services for pupils (f) Outside activities (g) Services to parents (h) School management and administration
B Support of children in schools maintained by other local authorities or in independent schools	(a) Extra-district pupils (b) Assistance to pupils in independent schools

Secondary education

Elements	Sub-elements
A Maintaining schools	(a) Accommodation (b) Teaching (c) Support for teaching (d) Buildings and grounds (e) Services for pupils (f) Outside activities (g) Services to parents
B Support of children in schools maintained by other local authorities or in independent and direct grant schools	(a) Extra-district pupils (b) Assistance to pupils in independent and direct grant schools

Or, reversing the basis of subdivision, we might present the Further education programme category in this way:

Programme category: Further education

Elements	Sub-elements
A Teacher training	(a) Promoting the education of the authority's students locally and elsewhere (b) Providing colleges of education
B Higher education and advanced further education	(a) Promoting the education of the authority's students (b) Providing colleges
C Non-advanced further education	(a) Promoting the education of the authority's students (b) Providing colleges

Still further subdivisions are possible (and indeed will be necessary). For example the teacher-training element above could be further subdivided on the same pattern as the schools' programme categories:

Programme category: Further education

Element	Sub-element	Components
Teacher training	Providing colleges	(i) accommodation (ii) teaching (iii) support for teaching (iv) buildings and grounds (v) services to students (vi) outside activities (vii) college government and administration

Again there is no one correct way of proceeding from categories to elements, thence to sub-elements, and so forth. It is a matter of convenience, a process of trial and error. Thus reverting to the primary education programme category we might think the following pattern useful:

Programme category: Primary education

Elements	Sub-elements	Components
A Maintaining schools	(a) Infant education	(i) accommodation (ii) teaching (iii) support for teaching (iv) buildings and grounds (v) services to pupils (vi) outside activities (vii) school management and administration
	(b) Junior education	(i) accommodation (ii) teaching, etc.
B Support of children elsewhere	(a) Extra-district pupils	
	(b) Assistance to pupils in independent schools	

An alternative would be to make 'infant education' and 'junior education' the elements and 'maintaining schools' and 'support of children elsewhere' the sub-elements, thus:

Programme category: Primary education

Elements	Sub-elements	Components
A Infant education	(a) Maintaining schools	(i) accommodation (ii) teaching, etc.
	(b) Support of children elsewhere	(i) extra-district pupils (ii) assistance to pupils in independent schools

B Junior education	(a) Maintaining schools	(i) accommodation (ii) teaching, etc.
	(b) Support of children elsewhere	(i) extra-district pupils (ii) assistance to pupils in independent schools

By making the change we can see the kind of effect transpositions like this can have. The most immediately obvious result is to divide, perhaps unnecessarily, 'support of children elsewhere' into infant and junior categories. Another more serious but less immediately obvious defect would be, however, to divide completely the programme category in relation to providing accommodation for infant and for junior pupils. Yet it may often be necessary to house infants in junior schools: indeed many primary schools, particularly in rural areas, are designed for infant and junior pupils. The same objection would also apply to the pattern on p. 69 in which 'infant education' and 'junior education' are sub-elements. So this superficially helpful division may in practice be better left out. The fact is that it is not always a necessary division in our thinking about primary education. It has significance in relation to such things as the type of training needed by teachers, the size of desks and (wrongly) the amount of money per pupil authorities spend, but not in relation to such matters as the number of pupils per teacher. If then we make subdivisions in the programme structure only where the need arises, we shall differentiate between junior and infant education only as subdivisions of sub-elements.

Applications

To some this detached and somewhat esoteric probing into the programme structure may perhaps appear daunting. To others it may appear a superficial tinkering with inessentials. It seemed to me necessary, however, to illustrate the kind of process needed to get a programme-planning exercise off the ground.

It should at least demonstrate what a programme structure is for. We can see, for example, how the structure may be a help or a hindrance to thinking about objectives and to allocating resources to them; both are essential parts of PPBS. So far as objectives are concerned the structure may positively influence their identification and thus, in a sense, what they become. Whether the pattern is client-centred or activity-centred it should help to shift attention from maintaining institutions as an end in itself and to focus it on the reasons for their existence.

The complexities of programme structuring are, of course, reduced if the programme area is that of a school or college rather than a local education authority. For the individual institution the pattern could be a relatively simple one. For example:

Programme	Programme categories
Primary education in Central Street County Primary School	1 Accommodation 2 Teaching 3 Support for teaching 4 Buildings and grounds 5 Services for pupils 6 Outside activities 7 School management and administration

Even so, however, subdivision into elements will almost certainly be needed. For example:

Programme category	Elements
1 Accommodation	A School population B Organisation of classes C Quality of accommodation
2 Teaching	A Supply of full-time teachers B Part-time and visiting teachers C Pupils' attainments D Quality of teaching (a) qualification (b) in-service training (c) curriculum development
3 Support for teaching	A Personnel (a) aides (b) clerical (c) ancillary B Physical (a) books, stationery and materials (b) machine aids (c) audio-visual equipment

The full significance of the programme structure becomes clearer when the planning exercise is carried through its later stages. At this point we are concerned to achieve a subdivision that will help in the identification and clarification of objectives, a process we shall consider more closely in the next chapter.

8 Programme statements
(II) Objectives

No one will need reminding that agreement on meaningful objectives for education is difficult. Generally speaking, the broader and vaguer one's statement of objectives, the more the agreement with it, but the less the practical use that can be made of it. Conversely, the more specific and useful the statement, the fewer the people who will accept it.

There is no point, however, in objectives so vague that everyone can agree on them. A general objective for an education authority would likely to be of that kind, so I shall make no attempt to suggest one here. A more promising starting-point might be to identify an objective for each of the programme categories suggested in chapter 7. Even then the value would be that of indicating general directions rather than specifying particular targets. Those set out here are not suggested as ideals: they are based, in fact, on the first thoughts of a number of groups of specialists in an education authority that was undertaking a PPBS review.

Objectives for programme categories

Pre-school education

Providing and promoting activities designed to care for young children and to prepare them for school, including:
(a) securing the provision of adequate resources for nursery education for children aged between two and five years, particularly those with social, environmental or other handicaps:
b) ensuring that all privately owned nursery facilities and child-minding organisations conform to accepted standards of provision;
(c) promoting voluntary interest and activity in supporting these objectives; and
(d) assisting the health authority to provide child care in day nurseries devoted to the needs of children aged from nought to five years who might otherwise suffer handicap or neglect.

Primary education

Developing the potential of every individual, physically, intellectually, aesthetically, emotionally, practically and socially. For this it is necessary to:

(a) provide teachers in sufficient numbers and quality;
(b) support them adequately by ancillary staff;
(c) provide adequate buildings within reasonable distance of where children live, particularly infants;
(d) provide adequate equipment, books and materials;
(e) encourage co-operation between teachers, parents and school managers;
(f) ensure a smooth transition from primary to secondary school;
(g) pay particular attention to the needs of children for whom primary education must seek to compensate for social, environmental and other handicaps; and
(h) assist pupils to attend where necessary institutions provided by other bodies.

Secondary education

Promoting the personal, social and educational development of each pupil to his, or her, fullest potential by:
(a) providing public education for the authority's children at the secondary stage of full-time education (presently those between the ages of eleven and fifteen and those older children who wish it) according to their age, abilities and aptitudes, by ensuring sufficient and appropriate provision of school buildings and associated facilities, staff and equipment;
(b) taking places in schools maintained by other local authorities or bodies for pupils where the claims of parental choice and/or the recognition of particular educational considerations are accepted; and
(c) giving appropriate support to pupils in the authority's schools and elsewhere.

Children with special needs

Helping, through education, children with any form of handicapping condition or circumstance to become mature and competent members of the community and to enjoy satisfying, purposeful and positive lives, having regard to their personal, social and vocational abilities and aptitudes.

Meals and milk

(a) Providing a well-balanced, nutritional, midday meal within approved cost limits for all children (i) on payment by those whose parents wish to avail themselves of the service and (ii) without charge for those entitled to receive a free meal because of the parents' economic circumstances;

F

(b) serving the meal in good conditions at the individual schools;
(c) providing additional meals at residential schools and colleges; and
(d) providing refreshments according to student requirements in further education establishments.

Further education

(a) Promoting the further education of all the authority's citizens who are over statutory school-leaving age and providing financial support to enable them to pursue their studies; and
(b) providing colleges and institutions of further education to meet the needs of the authority, and to share in meeting the needs of the region and the country as a whole.

Social, cultural and recreational education

(a) Promoting and providing informal social, cultural and recreational education for (i) young people, mainly between the ages of fourteen and twenty-one, (ii) younger children and (iii) adults;
(b) promoting and providing more formal, non-vocational, adult education.

Youth employment service

Helping young people to make sound career choices so that, on completing their schooling, they can develop to the utmost their potentialities through work, training and further education, consistent with local and national needs and opportunities.

It is clear that none of these in themselves would be of great value in, say, devising a programme budget or working out an action programme: they are still too broad. In some cases (for instance, Primary education) to help overcome this, a number of particular activities have been specified. It is arguable that this is an aid to clarifying thought and therefore to be commended. We should bear in mind, though, that these are means not ends, so that without greater refinement of the objective itself there may be danger of perpetuating the kind of habitual thinking this new planning process is designed to challenge.

It is worth looking a little more closely at the implications. Does providing teachers in itself guarantee the achievement of the very lofty ideals of the Primary education programme category, for example? The reference to 'sufficient numbers' is a reminder that we are seeking a suitable staff–pupil ratio in terms of cost–effectiveness, not an automatic increase which assumes that one teacher for each pupil is the ideal. The reference to quality indicates that the nature of what is taught and the way it is handled are important, too. If we are to do more than scratch the surface in our analysis we must be more specific about the ends we want to achieve: we must try to turn general statements like 'sufficient numbers' into specific ones and we must be clear about the basis on which we do so.

Identifying objectives

This is where refining the programme structure is of value, for it helps to identify the needs of the community for whom we are planning. Much of our social planning begins, very properly, from negative goals. We may not find it easy to put into words (still less action programmes) our objectives for social justice, but we can probably make a much better attempt at stating what injustices we hope to remove.

Now it would be neither useful nor seemly for me to pontificate about objectives in the various parts of the education service. These are to be worked out collectively in relation to the needs of particular areas or particular schools or colleges at particular moments of time. There are no tablets to be handed down from the mountain top. What may be useful, however, is a more detailed breakdown of the activities of the education service to try to identify points at which relevant objectives need to be formulated.

The following pages, therefore, set out a possible programme structure for the whole of an LEA programme area. Readers may, if they have time and patience, try to work out more precise objectives for each sub-element in the structure. The activities or components suggest the range such objectives might cover and the inadequacies they might help to eradicate.

Table 2 **Identifying objectives through programme structure**

1 Pre-school education: Programme category

Elements	Sub-elements	Activities
A Provision by LEA	(a) Nursery schools	(i) Identification of need
		(ii) Provision of places
		(iii) Premises
		(iv) Staffing
		(v) Equipment
	(b) Nursery classes	(i) to (v) as above
B Assistance to other bodies	(a) Links with health department	(i) Identification of need
		(ii) Day nurseries
		(iii) Other
	(b) Aid to voluntary bodies	(i) Private nurseries
		(ii) Child-minders
		(iii) Pre-school play groups

2 Primary education: programme category

Elements	Sub-elements	Components
A Primary education in maintained primary schools	(a) Accommodation	(i) Population
		(ii) Organisation patterns
		(iii) Quality
		(iv) Educational priority
	(b) Teaching	(i) Supply and distribution of teachers
		(ii) Remedial teachers
		(iii) Pupils' attainments
		(iv) Quality and standards in teaching
		Training
		college secondment
		in service
		external courses
		Recruitment
		Selection and appointment
		Probation
		Promotion
		Advice and inspection
		Curriculum development
		Teachers' advisory committees
		Teachers' societies
	(c) Support for teaching	(i) Personnel
		Aides including technical
		Clerical
		Supervisory
		(ii) Physical
		Books, stationery and materials
		Mechanical aids
		Audio-visual equipment
	(d) Buildings and grounds	(i) Design and improvement
		New building
		Furniture
		Alterations
		Playing fields
		(ii) Maintenance
		Caretaking and cleaning
		Cleaning equipment and materials

Elements	Sub-elements	Components
		Heat, light and water Painting Repairs Furniture Upkeep of grounds (iii) Rents and Rates Outgoings Receipts (iv) Debt charges
	(e) Services for pupils	(i) Pupil movement (ii) Allocation (iii) Aids to pupils Clothing and footwear Maintenance grants Travel home to school other (iv) Welfare Boarding education Special services (v) Evaluation Record cards
	(f) Outside activities	(i) Educational visits (ii) Museum education service (iii) Theatre, music and the arts (iv) Physical recreation (v) Swimming (vi) Transport
	(g) Services to parents	(i) Home and school links (ii) Consultation and complaints
	(h) School management and administration	(i) Managing bodies (ii) Administration Secretarial Record keeping Stationery, postage, telephones, etc.
B Support of children in schools maintained by other authorities or in independent schools	(a) Extra-district children (b) Assistance to pupils in independent schools	(i) To other authorities (ii) From other authorities (i) Fees (ii) Boarding grants

3 Secondary education: programme category

Elements	Sub-elements	Components
A Secondary education in maintained secondary schools	(a) Accommodation	(i) Population
		(ii) Organisation patterns
		(iii) Quality of accommodation
	(b) Teaching	(i) Supply and distribution of teachers
		(ii) Categories of teachers Remedial Pastoral, including careers Specialist subjects Other
		(iii) Pupils' attainments

		(iv) Quality and standards in teaching
		Training
		  college
		  secondment
		  in-service
		  external courses
		Recruitment
		Selection and appointment
		Probation
		Promotion
		Advice and inspection
		Curriculum development
		Teachers' advisory committees
		Teachers' societies

	(c) Support for teaching	(i) Personnel Aides including technical Clerical Supervisory
		(ii) Physical Books, stationery, material Mechanical aids Audio-visual equipment
	(d) Building and grounds	(i) Design and improvement New building Furniture Alterations Playing fields
		(ii) Maintenance Caretaking and cleaning

Elements	Sub-elements	Components
		Cleaning equipment and materials
		Heat, light and water
		Painting
		Repairs
		Furniture
		Upkeep of grounds
		(iii) Rents and Rates
		Outgoings
		Receipts
		(iv) Debt charges
	(e) Services for pupils	(i) Pupil movement
		(ii) Counselling
		(iii) Aids to pupils
		Clothing and footwear
		Maintenance grants
		Travel
		home to school
		other
		(iv) Welfare
		Boarding education
		Special services
		(v) Evaluation
		Record cards
		Public examinations
		Sixth-form choice
	(f) Outside activities	(i) Educational visits
		(ii) Museum education service
		(iii) Theatre, music and the arts
		(iv) Physical recreation
		(v) Swimming
		(vi) Pupils' courses
		(vii) Transport
	(g) Services to parents	(i) Home and school links
		(ii) Consultation and complaints
	(h) School government and administration	(i) Governing bodies
		(ii) Administration
		Secretarial
		Record keeping
		Stationery, postage, telephones, etc.
B Support of children in schools maintained by other authorities, or in independent and direct grant schools	(a) Extra-district pupils	(i) To other authorities
		(ii) From other authorities
	(b) Assistance to pupils in independent and direct grant schools	(i) Fees
		(ii) Boarding grants

4 Children with special needs: programme category

Elements	Sub-elements	Components
A Identification of needs	(a) Detection (b) Assessment (c) Diagnosis	
B Treatment: direct provision	(a) Children with intellectual handicap	(i) Accommodation (ii) Teaching (iii) Support for teaching (iv) Buildings, etc. (v) Services for pupils (vi) Outside action (vii) Services to parents (viii) School government and administration
	(b) Children with emotional and behaviour handicap	(i) to (viii) as above
	(c) Children with physical handicap	(i) to (viii) as above
	(d) Socially deprived children	(i) to (viii) as above
C Treatment: links with other bodies	(a) to (d) as above	(i) Payments to other authorities (ii) Grants to individuals (iii) Joint projects

5 Further education: programme category

A Teacher training	(a) Promoting the education of authority's students	(i) Awards to students (ii) Pool contribution (iii) Salaries of seconded teachers (iv) In-service training for teachers and assistance for courses
	(b) Provision of colleges of education	(i) Number of students Demand Utilisation of existing resources (ii) Quality and output of teaching Staff/student ratios Students' attainments Recruitment Selection and appointments Promotion In-service training and secondment Courses/conferences

Elements	Sub-elements	Components
		Advisory service
		Advisory committees
		(iii) Services to students
		Information
		Welfare
		Lodgings
		Other
		(iv) Premises and grounds
		Buildings and furniture
		Provision and design of new buildings
		Alterations
		Maintenance
		(v) Government and administration
		Governing bodies rules and servicing
		Administrative staff
		(vi) Establishment expenses
		Debt charges
		Central administrative charges
		(vii) Income
		Teacher training pool reimbursement
B Higher and advanced further education	(a) Promoting the education of the authority's students	(i) University awards
		(ii) Advanced further education awards
		(iii) Advanced further education pool contribution
	(b) Provision of colleges	(i) Number of students
		Demand
		Inter-authority arrangements
		Utilisation of existing resources
		(ii) Establishment expenses
		(iii) Income
		Tuition fees
		Pool reimbursement

Elements	Sub-elements	Components
Internal programme structure for a polytechnic		
I Teaching	(a) Full-time courses	(i) Student contact
		(ii) Assessment
		(iii) Policy-making
		(iv) Staff development
	(b) Part-time courses	(i) to (iv) as above
II Support for teaching	(a) Library	(i) Technical staff
		(ii) Other staff
		(iii) Equipment
		(iv) Materials
	(b) Computer	(i) to (iv) as above
	(c) Educational technology	(i) to (iv) as above
III Research	(a) Externally sponsored	(i) Staff
		(ii) Equipment etc.
		(iii) Accommodation etc.
	(b) Internally sponsored	(i) to (iii) as above
IV External relations	(a) Information	(i) Staff
		(ii) Other
	(b) Community service	(i) and (ii) as above
V Premises	(a) Teaching	(i) New provision
		(ii) Maintenance
		(iii) Furnishing
	(b) Communal	(i) to (iii) as above
	(c) Residential	(i) to (iii) as above
VI Student & staff services	(a) Guidance & welfare	(i) Health
		(ii) Counselling
		(iii) Appointments
		(iv) Accommodation
		(v) Religion
	(b) Recreation	(i) Physical
		(ii) Other
		(iii) Students' Representative Council
	(c) Financial aid	(i) Scholarships
		(ii) Loans
	(d) Catering	(i) Routine
		(ii) Special
VII Administration	(a) General	(i) Committees
		(ii) Office services
		(iii) Travel
		(iv) Hospitality
	(b) Establishment	(i) Advertising
		(ii) Interviewing
		(iii) Processing
	(c) Registration	(i) Advertising
		(ii) Student services

Elements	Sub-elements	Components
C Non-advanced further education	(a) Promoting the education of authority's students	(i) Awards (ii) Inter-authority payments (iii) No-area pool contribution
	(b) Provision of colleges	(i) Number of students Demand Inter-authority arrangements Admissions policy Utilisation of existing resources (ii) Courses Distribution, type, grading Fee structure (iii) Quality and output of teaching Staff/student ratios Students' attainments Recruitment Selection and appointments Promotion In-service training and secondment Courses/conferences Advisory service Advisory committees (iv) Support for teaching Technical assistance Books, stationery and materials Teaching aids (v) Educational equipment (vi) Services to students Information Examinations: college-based and external Welfare Lodgings Outside activities Student health service Students' unions

Elements	Sub-elements	Components
		(vii) Premises Buildings and furniture Provision and design of new buildings Hostels, common rooms and amenities Alterations Hiring Security Grounds Rent and rates Maintenance
		(viii) Government and administration Governing bodies —rules and servicing Administrative staff
		(ix) Establishment expenses Debt charges Central admin. charges
		(x) Income Tuition fees Inter-authority repayments No-area pool reimbursement

6 Meals and milk: programme category

Elements	Sub-elements	Components
A I Provision of meals	(a) Pupils' meals	(i) General (ii) Free (iii) Older pupils
	(b) Staff meals	(i) Assessment of need (ii) Provision
	(c) Holiday meals	(i) Assessment of need (ii) Distribution
	(d) Meals in residential establishments	(i) Numbers (ii) Special requirements
II Accommodation	(a) Central dining rooms	(i) Premises (ii) Furniture and equipment
	(b) School dining rooms	(i) Premises (ii) Furniture and equipment
III Production facilities	(a) School kitchens	(i) Premises (ii) Equipment

Elements	Sub-elements	Components
	(b) Pre-cooking facilities	(i) Premises (ii) Equipment
IV Staffing	(*List categories*)	(i) Recruitment (ii) Training
V Transport	(a) Vehicles (b) Accommodation	

B Milk

C Further education meals

7 Social, cultural and recreational education: programme category

Elements	Sub-elements	Activities

A Youth service	(a) Direct provision	(i) Provision of opportunities for membership of clubs and groups
		    According to age
		        5–14
		        14–18
		    According to areas of social needs
		(ii) Provision of premises
		    Purpose-built
		    Use of schools
		(iii) Provision of leaders
		    Full-time
		    Part-time
		    Instructors
		(iv) Leadership training
		    Training centres
		    Financial assistance for courses
		(v) Special facilities
		    Counselling
		    Outdoor pursuits
		(vi) Administrative and advisory services

	(b) Assistance to voluntary bodies	Categories as above
B Community service	(a) Direct provision (b) Assistance to voluntary bodies	Categories as above Categories as above

C Adult education	(a) Direct provision	(i) Centres
		    Evening institutes
		    Other centres
		(ii) Staffing
		    Recruitment, etc.
		    Training

Elements	Sub-elements	Activities
	(b) Assistance to voluntary bodies	(i) University extra-mural (ii) WEA (iii) Other

8 Youth employment service: programme category

Elements	Sub-elements	Activities
A Careers information and advice	(a) Careers guidance	(i) Group work Group talks Group discussion Lunch hour guidance (ii) Individual work Personal interviews Discussion with parents
	(b) Information service	(i) Visits to employers (ii) Job studies (iii) Careers conventions (iv) Careers guide (v) Careers teachers' associations (vi) Talks to parents (vii) Representation on joint apprenticeship committees, group training associations. etc. (viii) Contacts with industry training boards (ix) Contacts with colleges of further education and University Appointments Board
	(c) Liaison with careers teachers	(i) Careers library (ii) Careers conventions (iii) Specialist speakers and panels (iv) Industrial visits (v) Work experience (vi) Careers teachers' associations (vii) Materials may include films, film-strips, radio and television

Elements	Sub-elements	Activities
B Employment	(a) Job finding	(i) Notification and circulation of vacancies
		(ii) Job knowledge
		(iii) Knowledge of employers
		(iv) Surveys of local industry
		(v) Opportunities outside area
		(vi) Training allowances scheme
		(vii) Register new entrants to national insurance under age 18
		(viii) Register unemployed
		(ix) Statistical information and returns to Department of Employment and Productivity
	(b) Review of progress	(i) Invite young workers
		To office
		To former school
		(ii) Visit youth clubs
		(iii) Home visits
		(iv) Special cases, e.g. approved schools, handicapped, care and protection cases
		(v) Enquiries on visits to employers
C Agency Services	(a) Registration	
	(b) Payments of benefits and allowances	
D Special Needs	Handicapped pupils	Additional Activities
		(i) Collaborate with school medical officers and other specialists
		(ii) Case conference before school-leaving
		(iii) Refer cases to further education department in cases needing financial assistance for special courses of further education and training

In so fundamental a matter as that of establishing objectives there is no substitute for hard, individual thought. And even the hardest and most prolonged thought is unlikely to produce anything like perfection. It can be a labyrinthine process, with one argument leading to a counter-argument and, sometimes, one benefit seeming to be offset by a disadvantage at almost every stage. So, although it is important to ensure that this stage of the exercise is done thoroughly to provide a sound basis for what follows, we should be clear that scientific accuracy is not possible. Objectives can always be revised at a later stage as the various issues arising are analysed. What is needed at this point is a series of finger-posts to see that the exercise is directed towards achieving real, and not just assumed, ends.

Certainly it is not advisable to spend weeks and months striving after unattainable ideals of exactitude. It is sufficient to achieve an approximation such as that in the following example. This relates to a very small part of a local education authority programme concerned with the (philosophically) relatively simple task of providing accommodation for primary education.

Element	Sub-element	Components	Objectives
Primary education in maintained schools in Downshire	Accommodation	(i) Population	To provide premises to house all pupils having regard to the population and the social and environmental needs of the county
		(ii) Organisation pattern	To provide schools of adequate size to allow effective distribution of teaching staff and make educationally and economically viable units
		(iii) Quality	To provide buildings that meet modern educational requirements, including community use, and help to compensate for inadequate home conditions

The reader will doubtless discover imperfections of the grossest possible kind in these illustrations. As objectives (quite apart from any basic disagreement the reader may feel) they are still far from complete. They raise questions rather than answer them. They are, however, reaching the stage at which more precise *standards* can be set, quantifying such words as 'adequate' and 'viable'. This is a part of the exercise we shall pursue in the next chapter.

G

9 Programme statements: (III) Standards

At this point we must reduce the span of our attention. We have largely been considering the structure of the education service. In order to make progress we must now consider the texture of one or two selected elements in our programme. We must also move to some extent from description to evaluation. This is always difficult and with education it is especially so: evaluation usually implies some attempt at quantification; and in education many of the most important elements are hard to quantify. Even where quantification is not so difficult, as in such matters as accommodation, there are so many complex and interrelated factors—for instance, the link with staffing standards—that we are unlikely to produce a succinct and immediately compelling analysis.

Specific objectives

With this in mind we can move tentatively forward to the task of identifying specific objectives to which we can attach standards of achievement. In this it may be helpful to think of objectives as including three main components: first, *the activities* associated with a particular programme element (some of these were suggested in the previous chapter); second, *the clientele*, the people for whom the activity is undertaken; and third, the *purpose* for which it is carried out.

To illustrate this we can take the relatively straightforward aspect of the service—one that can to some extent be quantified—that of providing primary school places, taken as an example at the end of the previous chapter. The *activities*—relating to population, organisation patterns, quality of accommodation—remind us that just to provide a number of places is not enough. Our *clientele* is the number of children of primary school age in our area. The *purpose* is, of course to ensure suitable conditions in which children can learn.

We might set it out as shown at the top of p. 91.

The initial crudeness of the objectives is obvious. Let us look more closely, for instance, at that relating to population. It is important to an authority not only to have enough rooms for pupils but to have them in the right place: there is a limit to how far primary school children can be expected to walk or to be transported; parental choice has to be considered; admission zones may be needed; and so

90

Element	Activities	Objective	Clientele	
			1971	**1975**
Accommodation	Population	To provide premises to house all pupils of primary school age.	80,000 pupils	75,000 pupils
	Organisation	To provide departments of the best size to achieve an effective distribution of teaching staff in creating educationally and economically viable units.		
	Quality	To provide buildings suitable for modern educational requirements and community use.		

on. We may also, particularly since the Plowden Report, want to give special attention to the needs of children in educational priority areas. So the initial global statement of the clientele may need to be broken down, as in Table 3. (The pattern shows an overall decline

Table 3 **Primary school age children**

Area	1971	1975
		(est.)
1	8,000	6,000
2	11,000	12,000
3	9,000	7,000
4	12,000	12,500
5	10,000	10,500
6	12,000	12,500
7	9,000	7,500
8	9,000	7,000
	80,000	75,000

in population because of overspill from our hypothetical city to new housing outside it, together with a falling birth-rate. Within the city certain inner, decaying areas will decline in population, while other, suburban areas will increase.)

Assessing needs

This more detailed analysis of *clientele* is the beginning of a process that is central to PPBS. We have to know precisely for whom the service we offer is intended, as a step towards assessing needs. Often there is relatively little difficulty in establishing a specific clientele:

predicting secondary school populations from what is known of numbers attending primary schools has been raised to a fine art in most authorities, for instance. At other times, however, there are problems. Further education establishments have much less precise knowledge about the likely number of their customers. 'Schools for the educationally subnormal' are provided for 'educationally subnormal children' who may be defined as those who go to schools for the educationally subnormal. Youth clubs are for those who want to attend them on the particular occasions when they want to go.

In these cases we have to specify the *field of action* in which we are to operate. Perhaps this can best be clarified by an example outside education. The county surveyor for instance, in attempting an assessment of needs, can hardly be specific about the number of people who will travel about his county. He will seek other measures of his task: for example, the miles of road he has to provide. So too in parts of the education service it will be helpful to specify a level of provision: for example, the number of buildings that have to be kept in good repair.

Having established the clientele (or field of action) the next stage is determining the *standards* of provision required. The standards people strive to attain in education (as in the social services generally) are often implicit rather than stated. And, because of the nature of our system, it is not always clear who is entitled to specify standards. The discipline of a PPBS exercise, confronting us with the need to make explicit what is unspoken or assumed, may thus at this point be doubly valuable to us, however difficult it might be and however inadequate our efforts to cope with it. We cannot hope to improve standards and avoid waste of money if we do not accept this responsibility.

Once standards are agreed the remainder of the process is simple. *Standards* applied to *clientele* gives the quantitative *need*, which, compared with the present *provision*, shows up any deficiencies or surpluses. For example, assuming we set a standard of one teacher for every twenty primary school pupils, we might get the plan formulated in Table 4. Assuming then—a large assumption perhaps! —that there were agreement about the pupil–teacher ratio, we have an easy sum which, taken together with annual recruitment and wastage prospects, makes it possible to plan staffing needs over the next five years.

But there can be no doubt of the difficulties. Standards may be so general as to be meaningless, so idealistic as to be useless, or so inextricably interwoven with other factors as to make specifying them in isolation a very crude affair. Let us leave out of account, for the moment any special factors within the educational process

itself that might be thought to resist the application of tangible
standards, and return to the earlier example of providing accommodation for our primary school population. Let us forget questions

Table 4

Activity	Objective	Clientele	Standards	Needs	Provision	Deficiencies (−) or Surpluses (+)
Supply of teachers in primary schools	To provide sufficient teachers to meet the authority's needs in (a) 1971 (b) 1975	*1971* 80,000 pupils	Pupil–teacher ratio of 20 : 1	4,000 teachers	3,900 teachers	−100 teachers
		1975 75,000 pupils	Pupil–teacher ratio of 20 : 1	3,750 teachers	3,900 teachers in 1971	+150 teachers if 1971 standard kept

of quality or type of accommodation and concentrate simply on
classrooms (ignoring at this stage whether there should be enclosed
spaces called 'classrooms' in the modern primary school).

We might start off with a simple statement like this:

Clientele 1971	Standards	Needs	Provision	+ or −
80,000 pupils	Classes of 40	2,000 classrooms	2,600 classrooms	+ 600 classrooms

There is an immediate complication: the Standards for School
Premises Regulations specify a minimum room size of 540 square
feet for classes of forty pupils. So we should amend it to read:

Standards	Needs
Classes of 40 in rooms of 540 sq. ft and over	2,000 classrooms of 540 sq. ft and over

which might mean a variation like this:

Provision	+ or −
2,600 class-rooms, 800 of which are below minimum size	−200 rooms of minimum size

Furthermore, 'Classes of 40' is a very low standard. Could our
1975 standard be higher? Classes of thirty may seem impossibly

high in view of the serious shortage of accommodation we already
have. Yet the required minimum room size is less. So we might
find something like this:

Clientele 1975	Standards	Needs	Provision	+ or −
75,000 pupils	Classes of 30 in rooms 520 sq. ft and over	2,500; classrooms of 520 sq. ft and over	2,600 classrooms 200 of which are below minimum size	−100 rooms of minimum size

Superficially, then the new standard seems not only attainable
over a five-year period but easier to attain than classes of forty. And
so it might be, if it were simply a matter of building a hundred more
classrooms. We may find when we match accommodation against
school population, area by area, that in some districts we have a
surplus and in others a severe shortage. When the focus is narrowed
to the admission areas of individual schools the situation may be
still worse.

We could, theoretically, think of zoning our area so that pupils
were admitted according to the places available. This is what authorities must always to some extent do. But even if a satisfactory
arithmetical result could be achieved we cannot put the cart so far
in front of the horse. We need to look again at our standard, having
regard particularly to the three main dangers suggested earlier:
idealism to the point of uselessness, inextricable involvement with
other factors and generalisation to the point of being meaningless.
For one thing, 'Classes of ...' is meaningless. Pupils do not appear
at their schools in convenient groups of thirty-five nor can they
easily be dragooned into doing so. And even if they could, heads of
schools would be most unlikely to arrange them thus for teaching
purposes. A junior school receiving 105 pupils would be more likely,
given three teachers and three rooms, to make a smaller group for the
less able, giving classes of, say, thirty-eight, thirty-seven and thirty.
With a better ratio of teachers to pupils (and dislike of streaming)
there might well be some specialisation. Our 'Classes of 35' turns out
to be an average, which in the circumstances is not very helpful
as a target, for in setting such a standard in our school buildings we
are in effect saying that no class should have more than thirty-five
pupils. Consequently, if some classes are to have fewer than thirty-
five we shall need more rooms than the total number of pupils
divided by thirty-five.

Matters arising

The aim is to demonstrate a planning process, not to elaborate
upon the problems facing educators, so we cannot pursue the matter.

Our concern is with determining standards as part of the assessment of need. However, as the point has frequently been made that in this exercise much of the value must inevitably be in working through it rather than in any 'solutions' it may bring, it may be useful to try to show how even so rudimentary a part of the process opens up avenues of exploration. In the next few pages we shall see where this exploration takes us. It clearly has implications for school planning. The post-war emphasis on the flexible use of space in primary schools rather than on assembling collections of self-contained teaching boxes, has a bearing not only on educational methods but also on the efficient management of resources. Equally it has a bearing on staffing questions.

Heads of schools nowadays must concern themselves with both, must appreciate that the two go together. There is little room, and there will steadily be less, for the type whose idea of progress is bound by thoughts of more of the same. Surprisingly often the head who is suspicious of new-fangled open-plan schools is also unimaginative and unresponsive with regard to organisational innovations: he may resist having part-time teachers, for instance, because they complicate timetabling, and, more serious, he may be unable to think of other ways of teaching than facing the same teachers with the same groups of thirty or forty pupils throughout the week.

Though heads of this kind are fortunately few in number it would be wrong to assume that their attitude is on the way out. In spite of recent new thinking by the Nuffield Resources for Learning project, for example, there are negative influences at work. One is the concern of the teachers' unions to reduce the size of classes. Now this is, of course, a highly desirable, indeed long overdue, reform, but in the crude form in which it has tended to be expressed it is a potential threat to imaginative development of the service.

The teachers are scarcely to be blamed. Anyone who has ever worked for an LEA will know of the generally dismal approach to primary school staffing compared with that of the secondary schools. It is not merely that classes of forty have been thought acceptable for primary schools, compared with those of thirty for secondary schools, but that the concept of class-teaching in primary schools has for so long gone unchallenged. Indeed, it seems to have been implicit in national planning of teacher-supply.

Thus, since one of the ways of reaching an agreed standard is to adopt a national regulation or recommendation, the very first line of our planning exercise brings about a confrontation. The impracticality of the 'Classes of . . .' formula leads us to question the assumptions behind teacher-supply targets that have as their objective eliminating oversize classes.

The ninth report of the National Advisory Council on the demand for and supply of teachers between 1963 and 1986, was much preoccupied with this question and its findings were highly influential over a long period. (The reason can only have been that there was nothing else. It referred to a survey in London which suggested that a pupil–teacher ratio of 30·8 to 1 would make possible classes of forty or less, but then went on to give its own—unexplained—figure of 26·3 to 1 designed to do the same thing.) It was not until December 1968 that the DES stated that recent experience had thrown doubt on the validity of its assumptions. It is in fact impossible to equate any particular pupil–teacher ratio with any particular limit of class size, largely because of the freedom of heads of schools to dispose of extra teachers as they wish, such as in making smaller classes for the less able pupils.

That the DES nevertheless went on to accept 26·3 as a national target (thus conveniently providing us with an appropriate standard) by no means diminishes the lesson we can learn from this. The DES's reasons—that the target represented an improvement on existing standards—reminds us that there are no absolute standards in such things, no ideal pupil–teacher ratio, no point beyond which we need seek no more teachers! Instead we have to regard increases in the number of teachers available as one—rather costly—element in seeking to improve educational standards in a limited budget.

The corollary of this is that we should be sure that whatever teachers we have are deployed to the best advantage. It is right that heads of schools should be the best judge of this in relation to their own school, but equally the LEAs should claim a similar freedom in relation to the way they distribute teachers between schools. Thus a flat-rate pupil–teacher ratio, whether it be 26·3 to 1 or some other figure, though it may seem equitable, should, if the implications of the Plowden Report are accepted, be adjusted to give better ratios to schools in educational priority districts. There may then be a decision to be made on whether to aim at improving the overall standards of the authority or to concentrate additional resources on a few schools. The second course may not entirely accord with local authority traditions of fair shares all round or with teachers' union policies.

When our exploration is done we shall have to accept that the process of setting standards throughout the education service is certain to reveal many instances where arbitrary targets have to be set. However arbitrary they seem, they are in fact likely to be less so than in the past, for systematic spelling out of standards focuses attention on them and at least lays the foundation for later refinement.

Allowing for change

In setting standards, whether arbitrarily or logically, it is important to take into account any changes the future may be likely to bring. Five years ahead is usually about as far as is practical, and three may be better for many purposes. Significant developments, such as raising the school-leaving age, may make natural landmarks for particular programme categories. Sometimes, indeed, it may be desirable to show the effect of such events, both at the time and afterwards. This is the case in the example chosen to end this chapter (Table 5). Raising the school-leaving age has a marked effect on the analysis of the youth employment service's standards, needs and deficiencies. Like all the other examples it is not intended as an argument for the particular standards mentioned, but simply as an illustration of the process with which this chapter has been concerned.

Table 5 Statement of standards, needs and deficiencies: youth employment service

Activities	Objective	Clientele	Standards	Needs	Provision	+ or –
1 Careers and Information and advice	To give information and advice to secondary school pupils that will help them to choose a career	(a) (i) Pupils aged 13 and over 1970 1973 1975 34,000 39,000 39,000	Minimum of one group talk for every pupil before fourth year and subsequent contact	Group talks, etc., with pupils 1970 1973 1975 34,000 39,000 39,000	Group talks, etc., with pupils 1970 18,000	Group talks, etc., with pupils 1970 1973 1975 –16,000 –21,000 –25,000
		(ii) 100 schools	Careers literature packages in every school	20,000 books and pamphlets circulated	15 000 books and pamphlets circulated	–5,000 pamphlets circulated
		(iii) 100 schools	Careers conventions for every group of 5 schools	20 careers conventions	16 careers conventions	–4 careers conventions
		(b) 14-year-old age group 1970 1973 1975 10,500 10,500 10,500	Minimum of one personal interview with all 14-year-olds with parents present	10,500 interviews with parents present	7,500 interviews with 2,500 parents present	–3,000 interviews –8,000 parents
2 Assistance with obtaining employment	(a) To help young people under 18 get suitable jobs	School-leavers for employment 1970 1973 1975 8,000 3,000 8,000 (raised school leaving age)	(i) All leavers to be in suitable jobs within four months of leaving school (ii) All leavers to register for employment (iii) All vacancies to be notified by employers	Suitable jobs for 1970 1973 1975 8,000 3,000 8,000 Registration by 1970 1973 1975 8,000 3,000 8,000 In 1970 at least 7,800 vacancies could have been notified	1970 7,800 jobs, 6,200 of which were suitable Registration 1970 2,900 6,300 notified	1970 –200 jobs (–1,800 suitable) –5,100 registrations – 1,500 notifications

			1970	1970	1970
(b) To help unemployed young people find other work	Young workers under 18 1970 1973 1975 20,000 15,000 15,000 of whom up to 25% may register for re-employment	Re-employment of all who register	2,900 registered	2,000 found jobs	−900 new jobs
3 Service to employers	To assist employers to recruit suitable staff, provide information about educational methods, and to stimulate interest in providing training	6,300 employers in area	All employers to use services provided	6,300 to use services	5,400 use services	−900 do not use services
4 Staffing	To maintain high standards of service consistent with economy	One careers officer per 400 14-year-old pupils One careers officer per 200 handicapped pupils }	30 careers officers	27 careers officers	−3 careers officers
		Equivalent number of supporting clerical staff	30 clerical officers	34 clerical officers	+4 clerical officers

10   Programme statements:
(IV) Measuring impact

Having established standards of provision, however theoretical, we can, by applying them to the appropriate clientele, indicate needs. By comparing these needs with the actual provision made it is no problem to work out what deficiencies there are. It would be equally simple to follow this by compiling a list of the extra staff and buildings required to meet these deficiencies, and to end the matter there; but of course this would be to assume that the type of provision at present made is entirely effective. So to complete this part of the programme statement we have to try to measure the effectiveness of present performance.

In this we are concerned not so much with the effort put into the performance—though this may affect the outcome—as with its *impact*, the extent to which it achieves the underlying purpose of what is being done. This is a delicate stage in the operation, partly because it may arouse the susceptibilities of those doing the job and partly because it may require self-analysis or the ability to stand outside the situation and look at it objectively.

Achievement

It involves another look at the standards adopted, but this time in terms of level of achievement rather than level of provision. To have a certain number of teachers or of buildings may be a means to an end but it should not be confused with the end, nor should it be assumed that the end will be achieved because the means exist. Measurement of impact entails a careful look at how resources are deployed.

In this way the programme structure that has been compiled can be influential. With a good structure, the way certain factors interact with each other will be brought out. For example, as I suggested in chapter 9, an authority's pupil–teacher ratio is only as good as the way it is deployed. In the programme structure discussed there, one of the key activities, Organisation, had as its objective: 'To provide departments of the best size to achieve an effective distribution of teaching staff in creating educationally and economically viable units.' The standards set in this can help to ensure that the impact of improving pupil–teacher ratios is significant.

If we take the Plowden Report as our authority we can cite this (from paragraph 4.55): 'The advice of almost all our witnesses is that, with the present age range and class size, two-form entry junior or infant schools and one-form entry junior mixed and infant schools are the most satisfactory. An analysis of schools of special distinction showed that the national proportion of schools of the recommended size, exceeded markedly the national proportion of schools of other sizes.' A possible statement is given in Table 6.

Table 6

Field of action	Standard	Needs	Provision above standard	Deficiencies below standard
300 primary departments	Minimum size of 2-form entry junior 2-form entry infants or 1-form entry junior and infant	300 schools of standard or smaller number of larger schools	80 junior 78 infant 38 junior and infant ___ 196 ___	40 junior 44 infant 20 junior and infant ___ 104 ___

A school's size may be related to the extent of its premises, the numbers living in the area or its popularity with parents. As a first stage in securing the best deployment of teaching resources, then, we might profitably begin by considering whether to enlarge some schools or to impose admission zones or to cease to use certain buildings. This last possibility would depend on the results of the analysis under population (see p. 91) and this in turn would have a bearing on, and would be influenced by, an analysis under quality.

The process of ordered common sense, characteristic of PPBS as a whole, here casts light by the way it juxtaposes activities. It can cast light, too, merely by statement of the obvious. The basic questions it asks sometimes require answers so simple that they may have gone by default. When we consider, for example, another approach to measuring impact—assessing what is being achieved already by the various activities—surprising gaps may be revealed.

In how many authorities, for instance, has it been assumed over the years that 'there is no point in sending extra teachers to primary schools that have no rooms to make use of them'? Where this has applied, unless it has been accompanied by rigid zoning schemes limiting the numbers admitted to certain schools—and this is rare—the result has often been to ensure that schools that are the most crowded physically also have the worst staffing ratios.

We shall be wise if we do not expect too much of the method. Our hope should be to establish a framework within which illuminating comparisons can be made rather than to apply absolute standards. (This, of course, is again to follow the principles of PPBS as a whole. No one should expect to achieve perfect, or indeed any, 'solutions'.) The first stage of the process is simple consideration of what resources go into the activity concerned in relation to what the end-product is. And though this may give rise to all manner of detailed, even incisive, assessments, the standards of comparison used to initiate the process need only be worked out and tested sufficiently to enable them to be used as convenient points of departure.

By way of illustration we might begin with a criterion that is entirely naïve—measuring the success of a secondary school by the number of GCE passes it gets. Let us leave out of account the argument that 'exams are not everything' and accept for the moment that, in parents' eyes at least, they are something. As it is popularly applied the criterion is horribly unfair. A school with a good reputation tends to get the ablest pupils, who tend to get good results, which makes the school attractive to ambitious parents of the abler pupils, who are likely to get good results . . . And so it goes on, as does the reverse process with schools that no one wants to go to. Yet for an education authority to compare two schools as in Table 7 might be a salutary exercise.

Table 7   Numbers and costs of GCE O level passes

	Pupils	Annual cost £	Cost per pupil (£)	Nos. entered	No. of passes	Cost per pass (£)
School A	1,200	240,000	200	200	800	300
School B	1,200	240,000	200	200	600	400
or						
School C	1,200	240,000	200	200	1,000	240
School D	1,200	360,000	300	300	1,200	300

Two points must be made at once. A comparison like this is only the beginning of the analysis: all kinds of explanations and ramifications will (usefully) present themselves when such an exercise is attempted. And there is no question of judgment in making a comparison on this basis, no question of 'therefore school A is better than school B'. The idea is to enquire into causes and seek explanations using some crude measure of impact as a starting-point for this discussion, as a challenge to assumptions.

The second, slightly more sophisticated, example, (Table 8) takes as its measures of the impact of an LEA's secondary education programme (i) the numbers staying on at school after the statutory leaving age, and (ii) the numbers securing university and further education awards. This example is clearly representative of most aspects of the education service in that no single standard is likely to be accepted as a valid measure of impact. The more standards we can apply, therefore, to look at the situation from different angles, the better. The various measures may be used to cross-check each other.

Table 8

Standards	Provision in Mudby LEA	+ or −	Impact	Possible causes to be investigated
1 % staying at school after statutory leaving age: National average 1968:				1 Sampling: compare (a) county boroughs' average (b) average of boroughs of
15+ age group	50·4 44·1	−6·3	Performance	similar size
16+ „ „	29·0 24·7	−4·3	some 20%	(c) average of
17+ „ „	15·0 11·9	−3·1	below national	boroughs of
18+ „ „	5·2 4·3	−0·9	average	similar rateable
19+ „ „	0·5 0·4	−0·1		value (d) any special factors
2 % going on to (a) higher education and (b) further education (f.e.) National average awards 1967:			Performance some 30% below national average: in relation to universities some 37% below national average	2 Social factors (a) economic (b) other and compare with average 3 Staffing: compare with average (a) numbers
University	6·2 3·9	−2·3		(b) quality e.g.
Major f.e. courses	5·7 3·6	−2·1		qualifications
Minor f.e. courses	2·5 2·2	−0·3		(c) distribution, e.g. size of
Colleges o education	5·0 4·0	−1·0		schools 4 Organisation:
Total	19·4 13·7	−5·7		(a) grammar or comprehensive (b) size of schools, etc. 5 Costs: compare with national average 6 Individual schools: apply above criteria school by school

And in a process so closely bound up with getting value for money financial criteria must play their part. So we might begin comparing the impact of three colleges of education by looking at their costs, as in Table 9. It seems that the bigger college is more economical to run (and we could discover whether this is accidental or whether it is generally true of bigger institutions). However, if we were to apply another standard, that of results, we might get figures such as those in Table 10. There may, it seems be compensating arguments in favour of smaller colleges (another point to be checked to see whether this is a general or specific case). If we reapply financial criteria we find, interestingly, that the bigger college still does better in terms of cost per successful student over a three-year period, with college A at £2,760; college B at £2,622 and college C at £2,492. Of course we shall need to look into the reason for the higher wastage rate. We may find, say, that a substantial number of students who began the course transferred later to higher-level courses at the university or stayed on for a fourth year to take a B.Ed. degree. We may find, though, that the biggest proportion of those who fell

Table 9

	Clientele (students)	Standards	Need	Provision	+ or −	
		(1) Nationally recommended student-staff ratio		(Staff)		
A	460	10·5	44	46	+	2
B	480	10·5	46	48	+	2
C	920	10·5	87	88	+	1
		(2) National average cost per student (£)	(Annual cost per student) (£)			
A		656		720	+	£64
B		656		710	+	£54
C		656		650	−	£6

out found themselves, or were found by the college, to be unsuited to teaching. This may be evidence of high standards and extreme conscientiousness on the part of the academic authorities; it may mean that the selection processes are inadequate.

Yet we have to avoid the at least equal danger of drawing conclusions from this first stage. It is worth repeating that, at this stage

Table 10

	Clientele Nos. starting course	Standards	Need Passes	Provision Nos. of passes after 3 years	Impact successful (%)
College A	140	Theoretical: 100% success rate	140	130	92·9
College B	150		150	130	86·6
College C	320		320	240	75·0

at any rate, it is not a question of setting up criteria for deciding what is a good college and what a bad. A high rate of drop-out may after all indicate no more than that there were few good candidates available for selection as students. The approach is rather that of input–output analysis. We consider first the out-turn, regardless of its cause. Thus, whatever the reasons, only three-quarters of the students starting at college C complete their course satisfactorily in three years; and it is legitimate to ask why and to see if the same outlay of resources could achieve a higher output by other means.

Evaluating performance

There inevitably comes a stage, however, when if we are to follow the logic of the method we have to go beyond this to consider, and try to evaluate, educational performance. Theoretically this too can be approached without any suggestion of apportioning praise and blame. Unfortunately the whole question has emotional over-tones of a daunting kind. Indeed in recent years it has bid fair to take the place of sex as an unmentionable topic.

Neither children nor teachers are supposed to have their per-formances evaluated: those who suggest it are thought to be insensitive reactionaries. So far as children are concerned the pendu-lum has swung from a ludicrous dependence on the eleven-plus test as a means of sorting out non-existent sheep from mythical goats to a feeling that measurement of any kind is inhibiting and somehow 'uneducational'. As to teachers, such is their apparent horror of a reversion to payment by results that they sometimes seem to acquiesce in a situation in which they are paid a pittance so long as no one tries to sort out good teachers from bad ones. All kinds of generalisations and half-truths are mixed up in this situ-ation: the false equation of educational opportunity with educational performance; the equally false equation of academic freedom with freedom from being accountable to the taxpayers; the reconcili-ation of the roles of professional and layman in educational govern-ment by a compromise in which teachers speak softly about political matters and committee members keep silent about what goes on in the classroom.

There is little to be gained by a few off-the-cuff pronouncements on this topic as a side-issue in a book about planning methods. What has to be said is that unless the education service takes seriously the question of measuring its own performance it will never be able to make out a satisfactory case for the resources it needs, nor use to the full the resources it is given. It is true that objective measure-ment of the educational performance of children, teachers or edu-cation authorities presents extraordinarily difficult problems, but the situation is made worse by the association of testing with the eleven-plus and the debate about comprehensive schools.

Do we even know how much time and money is actually spent in measuring children's performance at school? (We may suspect that it is a microscopic amount, but do we know?) Is it sensible to spend enormous sums on teaching and next to nothing on measuring

H

its effectiveness? How much attention do we give to researching new methods of evaluating performance?

It may be argued that the miserable history of the eleven-plus has scarcely encouraged further development of testing. This is true but scarcely fair. The worst features of the eleven-plus have little to do with the method of intelligence testing on which it is based. It cannot be too strongly criticised when it is used to make definitive pronouncements about what type of secondary school children should attend: two children whose test scores fall by small margins on either side of the borderline are much more intellectually alike than either of them are like those who score highest and those who score lowest. And the shrivelling effect on primary school curricula through excessive attention to the narrow range of tested subjects and to the slick methods required to score well in the tests has been a national disgrace for many years.

But these are the results of misapplication rather than inherent faults of the method. If IQ tests were used to predict what a pupil's performance ought to be and then compared with what he actually achieves they might prove much more valuable. To do this properly would, of course, involve a sophisticated analysis of how objective the IQ score really is: it has been estimated, for instance, that extreme environmental differences may affect test scores by as much as twenty points. But this in itself is a valuable exercise requiring the kind of research that an education authority intent on allocating its resources effectively and equitably ought to undertake.

The United States is less inhibited about this approach. One of the best-known attempts to produce better performance measures in education was the New York State Quality Measurement Project (QMP). The State Education Department tried in QMP to develop norms of achievement, suitably weighted to take account of environmental influences, through which local school boards could compare the performances of pupils in one district with those in another. The Educational Testing Service of Princeton was subsequently asked to develop a more comprehensive system on these lines for the State of Pennsylvania. The intention here was specifically to apply the results to a programme budget so that the State could decide what resources to allocate to the different school districts, and each district could measure the effectiveness of its programmes and see what needed to be done to strengthen them.

In British terms we might take as an example the implications of the Plowden Report. The Report (Section 551) states:

We have considered whether we can lay down standards that should be achieved by the end of the primary school, but concluded that it is not possible to describe a standard of attainment that should be reached by all or most children. Any set standard would seriously limit the bright child and be impossibly high for the dull. What could be achieved in one school might be impossible in another. With the ending of selection examinations some yardstick of the progress of children in schools in relation to others is needed. Without it teachers may be tempted to go on teaching and testing as they did before. It is envisaged, therefore, that some use will be made of objective tests and their norms can serve as a basis of comparison so long as teachers and others do not assume that only what is measurable is valuable.

We also think that there should be recurring national surveys of attainment similar to those carried out by the National Foundation for Educational Research in Reading and Mathematics.

These are unexceptionable sentiments, though perhaps the effort to make them unexceptionable has also made them vague. Presumably the 'others' who might join the teachers in assuming that only the measurable is worth anything include the LEAs. At any rate it is they, coming between the individual teachers and the national survey, who need to look carefully at their assumptions (which, so far from being what Plowden fears, often seem based on the belief that anything measurable is educationally speaking beyond the pale).

Suppose, for example, they accept one of the basic Plowden tenets—that the socially underprivileged ought to be given priority in the allocation of educational resources. How are they to implement this unless they attempt to measure both the standards of deprivation and the effects of any compensatory measures they may take? I know from experience that the natural reaction of administrators and teachers in many places was to go by hunch, or by comparison of bids from head teachers (again by hunch), or by the judgment of school inspectors or advisers. Now without in any way seeking to deprecate these traditional and indispensable techniques, I nevertheless think they should be supplemented, or tested, by more objective and systematic criteria.

If we take, for example, the kind of indicators suggested in Plowden it would be possible to extract from them measures by which different districts of an authority could be compared, such as the percentage of children resident in each district:

1 with major learning or behavioural difficulties (e.g. ascertained as suitable for special education),
2 receiving free school meals,
3 coming from broken homes,

4 who are members of large (six or more) families,
5 living in overcrowded houses, or
6 who are persistently absent from school without good cause.

These, suitably weighted, can be used to suggest which districts should have priority for improved staffing standards, pre-school education or new school buildings. Applied to individual school admission areas they can give an indication of the degree of disadvantage that children attending might be expected to suffer when considering the results of standardised intelligence or attainment lists. If the results coincide with those based on intuition, well and good: if not, then there is the basis for further investigation.

Plowden's remarks are, however, a necessary reminder that there are other kinds of evaluation than the quantitative. It would be beyond the scope of this book to go into detail about the relative values of the different methods or to list the points throughout the education service at which one or other might best be applied. But some of the possibilities are obvious: for example, the judgment of specialist advisers or inspectors, or the consensus resulting from an advisory committee report, or an *ad hoc* conference. And in the end the most effective, long-term performance measure of all is self-analysis.

The important thing is to see that where they are appropriate these measures are applied, and that when they have been applied their implications are considered. If this is to happen then the process must be systematic: the intuition of an inspector has little value if it is offered as an *ex cathedra* pronouncement. The preparation of a programme statement gives every opportunity for a thorough and organised appraisal of judgments of this kind, and offers a useful framework for an exercise in self-analysis.

Measures from outside the education service

So far all the measures we have considered have sought to apply educational standards. However, few if any educators are free from the need to justify their policies to people outside their own service. The resources provided for education are made available to some extent because education is believed to be a good thing, because it is the people's right, and so on, but the amount is very much conditioned by other factors, such as the presumed benefit to national prosperity. So it is no more than prudent to try to identify non-educational measures of the impact of educational programmes.

We might quote, for instance, the extent to which higher education courses meet specific manpower needs, or the way in which youth and community programmes reduce vandalism. This may offend those who fear a threat to academic freedom, but publicly financed education has always had to respond to the requirements of the society that sustains it. In the past the devoutness of the school's products might have been accepted as the main criterion; at any time since the Industrial Revolution the acquisition of vocational skills has been an accepted measure of success; more recently the growing economic strength of ordinary people has given weight to public demand for certain styles of education as a measure of what should be offered.

In practice, educators can generally safely use whatever extra-educational measures they can devise, secure in the knowledge that any resources allocated for specific, even narrow, purposes will almost certainly produce benefits of a broader, more liberal kind, simply because of the nature of our education system. Democracy, though a nuisance in terms of efficient administration, has its advantages. One might perhaps argue also that the quality and freedom of education is threatened just as much by the failure of educators to think through the implications of their policies as by malign external forces.

It is here where a system such as PPBS can help by confronting the educator with the logic of his assumptions. We might take an example from the Department of Education & Science's Education Planning Paper No. 1, *Output Budgeting* (1970). The Paper takes two things as the main objectives of nursery education: (i) to help the educational development and social adjustment of children below the compulsory school age, and (ii) to release mothers for work, especially those with scarce skills. Now I personally would dispute that the second is a sensible objective for nursery education at all, particularly since it would seem to clash with the need, now almost universally acknowledged, to give priority in pre-school education to disadvantaged children. As presented, however, it puts a point of view, and there is nothing in the way these objectives are set out to suggest that they are in any way incompatible. Significantly, it is only when what the Paper calls 'Measures or Indicators of Success' are recorded as part of the programme statement procedure, that the implications become clearer.

These measures are stated like this:

(a) Intra-educational
Assessments by teachers, inspectors, etc. of improvements in educational performance and social adjustment of children in compulsory schooling age range

(b) Extra-educational
Net increase in national income resulting from employment of mothers hitherto looking after their children

As a measure of success the extra-educational proposal seems, to say the least, esoteric: one hope the officers of the DES do not spend too much time chasing this will-o'-the-wisp. But, more important, the attempt to quantify and relate these two sets of criteria very quickly leads to questions (such as 'which children?') that show up weaknesses not merely in the measures but perhaps in the objectives. However desirable the objective of releasing mothers for work may be, it has little to do with any carefully thought-out educational provision: child-minding, perhaps, but you do not need trained teachers for that. No doubt if the outline in the Planning Paper were adopted as the basis of a PPBS system, these points would be subjected to rigorous scrutiny.

If we elevate the experience of this one example to a general theory the moral would seem to be that if extra-educational measures appear on analysis to conflict with essential educational purposes, then they should not be applied, even if this means a loss of revenue for the education service. In this case an extra-educational objective that would be compatible with the educational ones might relate to giving an equal chance to all children to start on equal terms (which can be argued in terms either of social justice or of economic sense—to avoid wasting money spent on later education). This would involve giving special attention to the preparation for school of children from families where their emotional and language development has been retarded or there are other intellectual, social and environmental handicaps. This would presumably include priority in nursery school places. So a reasonable measure of impact would be the proportion of nursery school places in districts of greatest social need, measured, say, by the indicators on p. 111.

Management information system

The need for indicators of this kind illustrates the value, argued in chapter 4, of an ordered management information system. In relation to an LEA programme statement that includes eight categories, with very many subdivisions into elements and activities, one that is probably being compiled by separate teams of teachers and administrators, it would be very easy for each group to adopt different units of measurement. Sometimes these may be necessary but often separate development is the result of chance.

The indicators are a case in point: it helps to ensure fair and objective assessment if the same pattern is used for the pre-school education, primary education and youth and community programmes as an aid to determining which areas should be given priority. Of course, in order to do this the area of the authority and its population needs to be subdivided. Again these subdivisions should be the same in all the relevant programme categories. (This may seem to be stating the obvious, but I can testify from personal experience that in one major PPBS exercise at least its obviousness only became clear midway through. Others may, therefore, profit from the suggestion.)

In Table 11, twenty areas were chosen, roughly equal in size, care being taken to include within them complete municipal wards as these were the basis of most social service data collection. Statistics relating to the six indicators of need were collected from the various departments and set out, on a separate sheet for each category, in an order of deprivation according to the number per thousand of the relevant group of the population. The appropriate weighting to give to each factor was carefully considered but, eventually, because the lists corresponded so closely to each other it was decided simply to total the six sets of numbers for each area and

Table 11   Areas of need: indicator scores per 1,000 of relevant group

Area	Large families	Over- crowd- ing	ESN and mal- adjusted	Free school meals	School absentee- ism	In- complete families	Extent of deprivation Total	%
1	92	155	66	93	56	78	540	9·0
2	45	88	79	84	49	83	428	7·1
3	58	84	70	61	52	64	389	6·5
4	83	75	71	55	43	56	383	6·4
5	75	49	83	74	46	32	359	6·0
6	49	83	56	64	50	46	348	5·8
7	54	60	47	69	46	43	319	5·3
8	53	28	93	60	51	33	318	5·3
9	65	37	45	48	49	38	282	4·7
10	35	42	48	49	44	62	280	4·7
11	33	79	37	32	39	39	259	4·3
12	34	28	52	41	44	48	247	4·1
13	46	43	36	38	41	31	235	3·9
14	38	30	27	32	42	44	213	3·5
15	30	20	28	32	45	51	206	3·4
16	20	32	43	25	46	32	198	3·3
17	28	19	17	39	52	42	197	3·3
18	35	3	23	22	39	42	164	2·7
19	37	10	22	24	36	21	150	2·5
20	26	17	8	16	31	29	127	2·1

to rank them. This proved a very satisfactory, broad-gauge measure for many aspects of the programme statement. When necessary, individual indicators were used: for example, those for free school meals in relation to the meals and milk programme category. And, of course, smaller subdivisions of the twenty areas, such as the admission areas of particular schools, were used where appropriate.

There is no need to labour the point: the basis is again that of ordered common sense. Standard subdivisions and indicators such as these, the standard layout of the programme statement itself and the documentation of the various stages, all combine to provide a framework in which comparisons become, if not easy, at least unencumbered by avoidable difficulties.

With the end of this chapter, then, we complete the survey of the programme statement. The survey has been conducted at some length because the discipline of a format in trying to focus attention on fundamentals is important to the success of the PPBS exercise. It is scarcely necessary to add that, in spite of its length, the survey has omitted a good deal. I have tried to include enough to give the gist of what is involved and to lay a foundation for individual exploration of the possibilities.

11 Action programmes:
(I) Programme budgets; goals

We have reached a stage in describing the planning process where the limitations of the narrative form present more than usual difficulties. It is possible to write—and to read—only one thing at a time; and in setting out the elements of a planning process it is highly desirable to recount them in the order in which they happen. In PPBS, however, there are difficulties in the way of doing this, for at various points several processes need to take place as nearly as possible concurrently.

Thus the summary in chapter 6 indicates that the *programme budget* can, tentatively, be started at this point. So it can: indeed in order

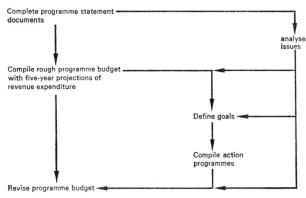

Figure 7

to get some idea of the levels of expenditure the evolving plans would require, it must be sketched. It may well be that finance committees or other allocating bodies will need at this point to know what is envisaged. Equally, having seen what is contemplated, they may in making their allocations create the need for a revision, a shifting if not a lowering of sights.

On the other hand, a reasonably precise and workable programme budget can only be devised after further detailed investigation of objectives, leading to identification of particular *goals*, and building them into *action programmes*. In turn, these programmes and thus the programme budget can only be laid down after alternative courses of action, different ways of achieving these goals, have been assessed, a process known as *issue analysis*. This in fact is a continuing process throughout the whole exercise.

Figure 7 gives an example of what should happen. To fit this into the necessary limitations of a narrative, however, I shall deal in the next two chapters with programme budgets and action programmes, leaving issue analysis for the final two.

The programme budget: purpose and format

The programme budget relates proposed expenditure to missions, that is activities with a defined purpose, rather than setting it out in conventional subdivisions. It is not just a rearrangement of sums of money but the application to the first-year programme in a long-term forecast of the results of a careful evaluation of priorities. At this point, though, we are concerned chiefly with the form it takes. First we should look at the conventional version.

To set out a complete, traditional, education authority budget would occupy many pages and would be highly repetitive. It is usually divided into separate sections for primary, secondary and further education, school meals, and so on, and for the purpose of illustration just one of these, primary education, will suffice (Table 12): the others adopt the same, or similar, subdivisions.

We should note that there are usually two annual budgets, one for revenue or recurrent costs and one for capital or once-for-all costs such as those of buildings or heavy equipment. Capital costs are commonly met by raising loans and the debt charges incurred are set against running costs in succeeding years. There are thus (from a planning point of view) two distortions: (i) the obscuring of the purposes for which money is spent by the categorisation chosen, and (ii) the inclusion of the effects of past capital expenditure. This second makes valid comparisons between current levels of expenditure and future proposals—the basis of conventional budgeting—extremely difficult. Expenditure and income are separately recorded, so that, except in the total figure for the whole education service, gross expenditure is usually considered, and it is not easy for any estimated income from a project to be set against its cost.

In contrast, the programme budget concentrates on the estimated costs of specific policies (i) by subdividing according to identifiable goals and (ii) by translating the capital cost of proposed new buildings and improvements into revenue terms. Also, expenditure is usually set out in net terms which means that true costs of a project can be measured by taking into account any income that may accrue to it. Furthermore it is given to the nearest £1,000 wherever possible to make comparison easier. A roughly comparable version of the traditional budget in Table 12 might look something like that in the left-hand column in Table 13 (though the traditional budget would be accompanied by a separate capital budget accounting for the cost

Table 12 **Traditional style revenue budget—primary education**

Expenditure (£)	Current year	Next year	Income (£)	Current year	Next year
1 *Employees*					
(a) Salaries and Wages			(a) Sales	2,500	2,500
Teachers	3,563,608	3,789,703			
Caretakers and					
cleaners	350,800	360,123	(b) Fees and charges		
Clerical staff	70,235	72,862	Violin class		
Aides	84,163	86,917	fees	260	290
(b) National Insurance	160,289	165,218	Parental contributions		
(c) Superannuation			Clothing	15	20
Teachers	270,319	284,163	(c) Contributions by		
Local government	8,300	8,850	other LEAs	153,649	243,106
2 *Running expenses*					
(a) Premises			(d) Rents	4,500	4,600
Repairs	165,000	135,000			
Painting	42,100	38,000			
Alterations	6,000	3,000	(e) Miscellaneous	50	50
Upkeep of					
grounds	84,629	88,279			
Fuel, light, water					
and cleaning					
materials	235,826	246,901			
Furniture	24,000	18,000			
Rent and rates	168,203	175,409			
(b) Supplies and					
services					
Books,					
stationery,					
materials	194,386	235,179			
Equipment	16,000	18,000			
Clothing and					
uniforms	2,700	3,100			
Laundry	4,200	4,400			
Transport	2,500	3,700			
(c) Establishment					
expenses					
Printing,					
postage, etc.	5,300	5,400			
Staff travelling	1,200	1,200			
Telephones	8,610	9,300			
Debt manage-					
ment expenses	3,205	3,319			
Other	2,869	2,961			
(d) Agency services					
By other LEAs	73,469	76,285			
By other					
committees	4,300	4,600			
3 *Miscellaneous expenses*					
(a) Educational visits	7,800	8,100			
(b) Aid to pupils					
Clothing and					
footwear	2,600	2,700			
Fees and					
expenses	2,850	2,950			
Travel: home to					
school	2,100	2,300			
Travel: other	12,500	12,500			
(c) Other expenses	2,275	2,368			
4 *Debt charges*					
(a) Interest	120,428	129,326			
(b) Redemption	111,301	114,609			
(c) Land Transfer					
Annuities	309	311			
Total	£5,814,374	£6,115,033		£160,974	£250,566

of proposed new building which in the programme budget is expressed in terms of its estimated annual revenue costs).

Clearly the schematic presentation in Table 13 would be of no use for any precise evaluation of priorities and ear-marking of funds. Its chief value lies in showing at a glance the proportion of expenditure that goes on the various activities. How sensible the distribution is will depend on a variety of things; for example, certain constraints

Table 13   **Primary education programme category**

Elements	Programme budget		Five-year projection of revenue expenditure				
	Current year total (£000)	Next year total (£000)	Additions or reductions proposed in future years				
			1 (£000)	2 (£000)	3 (£000)	4 (£000)	5 (£000)
1 Accommodation *	359	711	359	163	106	186	204
2 Teaching	4,143	4,146	3	4	−6	−8	−20
3 Support for teaching	183	243	60	80	100	100	100
4 Buildings and grounds	1,256	1,286	30	40	50	50	50
5 Services to pupils	3	4	1	2	2	2	3
6 Outside activities	49	52	3	3	3	3	3
7 School management	97	108	11	13	15	15	15
8 Allocated administrative costs	191	193	2	4	6	8	10
Total	6,281	6,743	469	309..	276	356	365
Less income from extra-district fees from other LEAs	−42	−46	−4	−6	−8	−10	−12
Total	6,239	6,697	465	303	268	346	353

* i.e. revenue costs of proposed new school places, improvements, etc.

—restrictions by the government or other sources—are built in, and in this the exercise of measuring provision, performance and impact should have shown up possible points for change. For this a more detailed breakdown along the lines shown in chapter 8 would be appropriate. However, the mere allocation of costs to heads of estimates is relatively simple, and the resulting layout, though easier for purposes of comparison and evaluation than traditional budgets, is not in itself an incisive planning tool. For this we need to turn our attention to the much more difficult phase of preparing action programmes.

Goals

The first stage is to fix goals for the various programme categories. These goals, as specific as possible, planned to take place over a period of years with specified action designed to achieve them, form the action programme. The process is in effect, the application of the standards discussed in chapters 9 and 10 to a time-scale and to particular methods of achieving them.

First the goals. Amongst the factors involved in defining them are

1 *the standards of provision*—including personnel, premises, organisational factors, equipment and so on—that will be shown up by the statement of standards, needs, deficiencies and surpluses (see pp. 93–9);

2 *output*, i.e. mainly productivity and efficiency: in this, output measures (showing, for example, the extent to which facilities are used, such as the number of students enrolled for adult education classes) are applied either alone, or, more usually, in relation to costs; measures such as cost per student or cost per successful student, may be useful yardsticks; and

3 *impact*, i.e. the estimated effectiveness of what is proposed, assessed by the direct and indirect measures that have been devised (see pp. 101–10).

It cannot be too strongly emphasised that the idea is not simply to list all the deficiencies in the service, cost them and spread out the extra costs of meeting them tidily over the succeeding five years. The measures of effectiveness, though harder to use, must be applied as rigorously as possible. We can perhaps most usefully illustrate this by outlining the results of a theoretical exercise in a part of the education service that we have so far said little about, that dealing with children with special needs.

The exercise began by sub-dividing the handicaps into four: learning; emotional and behavioural; physical and sensory; and social. Of these the largest category was that of children with learning difficulties. There was a substantial number of children in schools for the educationally subnormal, yet teachers complained that many children who should have been attending such schools were not doing so. Segregation into special schools is unpopular with parents and highly expensive so the programme statement set out to analyse the provision.

First an agreed level of educational subnormality was fixed: an IQ of below 70. (It was recognised that intelligence test scores, however skilful the testing, were subject to distortion from environmental influences; and also that an IQ alone is not an indicator of a need for special education. Yet some working standard was needed simply for the sake of theoretical analysis.) It seemed that by this standard some 1,500 of the 2,400 children concerned (or 62·5 per cent) were not in fact ESN: further investigation suggested that many of them were severely socially handicapped to the extent that their performance at school and in tests was as if they were ESN.

Two measures of impact were applied. About 1,600 of the children (⅔) were of secondary school age, which suggested that their condition, even if it had been correctly diagnosed, had been identified too late for them to be helped to make substantial improvement (and of course if the root cause of the trouble for many was environmental, as the first analysis suggested, and not innate lack of ability, substantial improvement could often have been expected). This led to the second measure of impact. Only 25 per cent of children admitted to special schools ever returned to the mainstream of education, whereas in view of the likelihood that environmental conditions had led to the admission of many such children a much higher rate of return could perhaps have been expected.

What seemed a further anomaly came to light. Assuming that the population of this authority was representative of the country as a whole in terms of intelligence, there should have been some 1,800 children with IQs between 50 and 69. But in fact only 900 of the children in special schools had IQs under 70, so that it seemed likely that about 50 per cent of children with very low natural intelligence had not been admitted to special schools. Investigation showed that, if they existed, they had not been brought forward for examination.

Hitherto the authority's policy had been directed towards expanding the provision of special schools, but now it seemed that these highly expensive establishments contained children who might be better treated elsewhere, and that in any event priority needed to be given to improving the process of identification and diagnosis. It also seemed that the needs of the seriously retarded would be best met by special remedial units attached to primary and secondary schools, and that others, retarded but less seriously, should be given more attention. The eventual statement of standards, needs and provision looked something like Table 14, and the eventual balance sheet of deficiencies and surpluses (much simplified) resembled Table 15.

Although therefore the overall cost of new policies was greater, the level of service was likely to be much higher, covering a much larger number of children: the cost per pupil treated would be much reduced. Furthermore, many savings were possible from discontinuing a number of special schools (which in practice became available for the new task of educating the severely subnormal (SSN) children, responsibility for whom was shortly to be transferred from health to education authorities). Above all, the standard of

Table 14 Children with learning difficulties (I)

Activities	Clientele	Standards	Needs	Performance/provision	+ or −	Notes
1 Assessment of children						
(a) Severely subnormal (IQ below 50)	500 (theoretical)	Identification by age 4	Identification of 550 by age 4	80 by age 4 20 by age 5 10 by age 6	−370 by age 4	All those referred for assessment were, apparently, correctly diagnosed. Process of referral needs improvement.
(b) Educationally subnormal (IQ 50—69)	1,800 (theoretical)	Identification by age 7	Identification of 1,800 by age 7	100 by age 7 100 by age 9 100 by age 11 600 in Special Schools were aged 12 or over	−1,700 by age 7	50% not identified at all: (i) less than 6% identified by age 7 (ii) referral still the main weakness, but diagnosis not so easy as with 1 (a) above
(c) Seriously retarded (IQ 70—79 but socially handicapped)	1,600 (theoretical)	Identification 50% by age 7 50% by age 12	Identification of 800 by age 7 of 800 by age 12	500 of primary school age in ESN schools 1,000 of secondary school age in ESN schools	n.a.	More difficult diagnosis: calculate (i) psychological services needed; (ii) nature of screening process in schools
(d) Retarded (IQs 80 and above)	8,000 (theoretical)	Identification 50% by age 7 50% by age 12	No formal process of identification	10 remedial teachers treating 800 children		
2 Treatment for children						
(a) Severely subnormal	550	Places in hospital or special schools	550 places	280 places	−270 places	At that time the responsibility of health authorities
(b) educationally subnormal	1,800	Places in special schools	1,800 places	2,400 places	+600 places	1,500 children attending had IQs above 70
(c) seriously retarded	1,600	Remedial units at primary and secondary school	900 places in primary 900 places in secondary	nil	−1800 places	A new approach adopted after issue analysis
(d) Retarded	8,000	Remedial teaching in ordinary school; 1 teacher per 200 children	40 teachers	10 teachers	−30 teachers	Augmented and organised version of present policies

Table 15 **Children with learning difficulties (II)**

	Deficiencies	Surpluses
Personnel		
Psychologists	5	
Teachers:		
In SSN special schools	(To be met by Health Department)	
In ESN schools		95
Remedial unit teachers	90	
Remedial teachers	30	
Buildings		
SSN establishments	(To be provided by Health Department)	
ESN schools		10
Rooms in primary and secondary schools	90	

performance, the impact, would be much improved: the cost per pupil *successfully* treated would be very considerably reduced.

In the light of this we can return to the process of setting goals. The technique is essentially that of providing a standard format for common sense, as a discipline. Thus we try first to clarify our particular goals under the three headings Provision, Output and Impact. Grossly over-simplified, this might be on these lines:

Provision

1 (a) 550 places in special schools for SSN children

(b) 1,800 places in special schools for ESN children

(c) (i) 900 places in primary school remedial units
(ii) 900 places in secondary school remedial units

(d) 40 remedial teachers in ordinary school system

Output

1 Cost per child: identification £x

2 Cost per child: treatment £x

Impact

1 100% identification of various categories by ages stated

2 At least ⅔ of children in ESN schools to be of primary age

3 At least 50% of children to return to ordinary school

4 Improved reading standards

These, together with estimates of expenditure on them over the planning period, in this case five years, should now be set out systematically. Again a standard format is important because the exercise will need to be carried out for each aspect of every programme

I

Name of activity written here	Current year estimated result	Planned for year 1	Planned for year 2	Planned for year 3	Planned for year 4	Planned for year 5
Goals						
Provision						
(a)...............						
(b)...............	(Specify	in detail)	(Less	detail required	for later	years)
(c)............... etc.						
Output						
(a)...............						
(b)............... etc.						
Impact						
(a)...............						
(b)...............						
(c)............... etc.						
Revenue costs						
Running costs, including staff						
Estimated revenue costs of capital proposals						
Gross expenditure Total						
Less income						
Total net expenditure						

.... **Programme category:**   **Element** ....   **Sub-element** ....

Figure 8   Programme plan document

category. That shown in Figure 8 is intended to be completed for each *activity/component* in the scheme in chapter 8.

These goals, the means of achieving them, the likely costs and the period of time it is proposed to take, are the main ingredients of *action programmes*. They will be discussed, together with some related matters, in the next chapter.

12 Action programmes:
(II) Priorities; expenditure projections

In practice, the analysis of issues, examining alternative methods of achieving goals, would be going on at this point in the exercise. As I suggested in chapter 6, this may well lead to a further refining, and even revision, of main objectives as a result of the light cast on them by an examination of their implications. However, so as to keep the complications to a minimum, this will be left for discussion in the next chapter, and we shall assume here that we have completed this satisfactorily, that we have settled the correct lines of action to suit our particular circumstances.

At this point, then, our concern is to translate our aims into practice. In considering action programmes we take into account such things as the time-scale for achieving our goals, and the assessment of how realistic it is. Sometimes the discipline of plotting the stages of a project designed to achieve a goal, may reveal hidden snags or weaknesses in the thinking behind a proposal: often it will reveal that it may not, in spite of appearances, be possible to complete a project by the time originally suggested. This can, of course, affect the programme budget and call for a revision of priorities. It can also increase the value for money we achieve.

Action programmes and priorities

Action programmes are not used exclusively in PPBS. They are a very useful standard tool of management that can be used for reorganisation schemes, policy changes, economy measures, new administrative procedures, and so on. Yet their basis of ordered commonsense is entirely characteristic of PPBS and as a check on the validity of proposals they can be invaluable.

An example of a pro-forma appears in Figure 9. Of course the form can be tailor-made for the particular enterprise using it: it is important, though, if the systems approach is to be sustained to have a standard format and naturally it is little use if the discipline it imposes is not strictly enforced. Apart from their value in ensuring that the task is precisely defined and understood, with each stage clearly set out, action programmes help in allocating responsibilities and give the co-ordinator a means of checking and controlling the progress of the various groups engaged in a planning task.

A particular value of the action programme discipline relates to timing. In all organisations, deadlines have to be met: a week's delay

Project _____

Stage	Whose responsibility?	What to be done?	By when? (Fill in dates)				Review	On what date?	What result?	Notes
			March	April	May	June				
1										
2										
3										
4										
5										
6										
7										
8										
9										

Figure 9 Action programme sheet

in bringing a project to a conclusion may mean missing a vital committee and lead to a whole year's delay. In planning, the experience of discovering that particular projects can take much longer than expected can, when part of an ordered system, lead to a review of priorities. It may be better, say, to substitute one project for another and thus get maximum value from the resources available. With an efficient system one can predict that a project is not likely to be completed on time and switch the allocated expenditure to something else. In a loosely organised approach, not only is the delay not discovered until too late but the experience is not put to good use for the future.

In programme planning it is essential that the priorities fixed should be projects that can be carried out in practice: otherwise the resources should be allocated elsewhere. Therefore the action programme discipline should be built up into experience that will make establishing priorities more than a vague indication of preferences.

Fixing priorities according to a time-scale is always important in planning. To educationists tackling PPBS for the first time it can be critical, for the initial production of a programme statement can lead to such a vast list of gaps in the service that it would be possible, say, to double the total expenditure on the service without making too much impression on the deficiency. And even when impact and performance measures have sorted out some of the dross the task can still seem insuperable.

Using a five-year time-scale can do two things. First, it can remind the planner that everything does not have to be achieved in the first year (one good effect of this may well be that the gap between the money our planner seeks and the money he actually gets may be less of a shock!). Second, as a corollary, it can make an apparently insoluble dilemma a little less intractable: to choose between twenty teachers for educational priority areas or a new nursery school may seem impossible, but the need to compile a phased programme presents new possibilities.

Two other documents are likely to be useful in establishing priorities: a capital project schedule and a manpower schedule. The first of these should set out—again adopting as nearly as possible the general style and pattern of the other planning documents—the different projects, building and equipment, planned for each year with their estimated costs. The second does the same for the personnel to be employed. Now the capital schedule is not in itself a programme planning document in the sense that it allows comparison of results to be expected from a given amount of expenditure. Nor is the manpower schedule. But they are extremely useful.

Essentially their purpose, like the time-scale in the priority programme, is to bring the planner up against reality. This reality may take the form of constraints—perhaps, for an authority, those imposed by the government, such as the limitations fixed by the annual building programme allocation, or by the quota of teachers; or, for a school, those imposed by the authority in, say, fixing its staffing establishments. Or it may be in the form of staff shortages—no use counting on ten extra psychologists, for instance, if they are unobtainable—or of the amount of output that can reasonably be expected from a given building firm in a year. These realities are of course part and parcel of the lives of most administrators and teachers. As planners, however, they have to build them into their calculations systematically.

Estimated revenue expenditure projections

When all this has been done we can return again to the programme budget. At this point it takes on a specific meaning: it is the first year of the five-year revenue expenditure projection setting out in relation to missions or planned projects the costs to be incurred. It is the basic justification for the resources needed to achieve what has been planned in the first year of a phased programme. Consequently it has to be compared with the current year's spending.

How this is done is an aspect of budgeting itself and to go into it in detail here would be out of place. If we have thoroughly carried out the various stages of the work outlined in this and the previous chapter, however, it is likely that we shall be able to improve considerably on the conventional presentation of estimates submissions. In addition to being able to divide the increases in expenditure we propose into the inescapable (arising, say, from salary increases) and the discretionary (for improvements), we can show more accurately how income may accrue or, even more important, what improvements in standards we offer. Furthermore, we may well be able to point to savings as a result of discontinuing certain activities or changing policies after our analytical review. And finally, whatever resources we are given, we shall be in a good position to see that the money is put to best use.

As I suggested earlier, programme budgeting emphasises revenue expenditure. Capital cost forecasts of course have their value because they identify specific proposals and highlight the process of choosing between alternatives. (Is it better, for example, to acquire a £25,000 piece of equipment for a college of technology or to establish a new child guidance clinic?) But in themselves they are not much use unless they show what implications spending a capital sum has for the revenue budget, so that all proposals, say for staff and buildings, can be looked at together as potential means towards achieving stated goals. Similarly the comparisons, difficult to make in any case be-

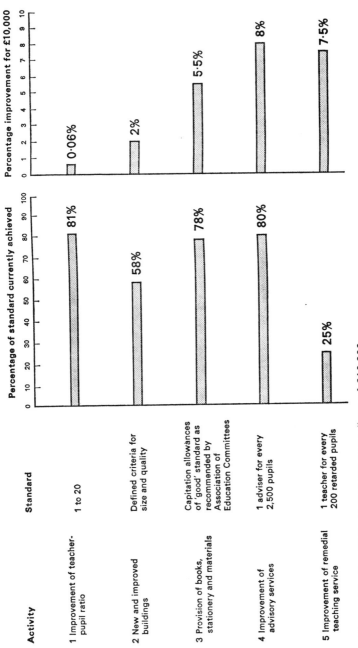

Figure 10   Sensitivity to revenue expenditure of £10,000

tween projects in different sectors of the service, are not valid unless they are made in net terms. For example, equipment provided in a further education college may bring in fee income (though of course the fees themselves may be paid by grants from public funds). Sometimes the comparison can be made easier by a sensitivity chart: that is a diagram showing (i) what provision is made by a number of activities, and (ii) the sensitivity of each of them to further expenditure. What will £10,000 buy in terms of equipment, teachers, etc. as a contribution towards achieving various goals? An example, solely for illustration, is given in Figure 10.

The projections should be presented as a five-year forecast, in detail for the first and in diminishing detail for later years. (The details are, of course, supplied in subsequent planning cycles as the horizon is pushed forward each year.) The simplest method is to plot them in (and on) the same form as that used for specifying the various goals, as shown in Figure 8. It will be seen that to give as realistic a picture of costs as possible the form allows for (i) the effects of capital projects on revenue costs, and (ii) any income that can be set against the particular activity. After the detailed schedules are compiled they can be summarised and the results presented as a general five-year projection to accompany the programme budget. (An example of such a projection is given in Figure 9.)

Summary

The detailed programme budget for the first year of the five-year programme marks the end of the first PPBS cycle. The cycle then begins again: revising programme structure; refining objectives; assessing performance and impact; assessing resources; fixing goals and converting them into action programmes; costing the programmes in a five-year revenue expenditure forecast; and, finally, producing a detailed programme budget for the new first year.

There is, however, a cycle within the cycle. From the outset, but more particularly from the point at which goals are beginning to be fixed, the process of issue analysis has an important influence on the system. Indeed the quality of the issue analysis in large measure determines the quality of the whole exercise. The ordered pattern outlined above can be of great value in prompting systematic review of existing practices as a basis for planned allocation of resources; but it is, in a sense, one-dimensional without the exploration in depth of the issues, great and small, that the process brings to light. The extra dimension will be considered in the remaining chapters.

13 Analysing issues

The word 'issue' has quite a few meanings. Here we must give it a rather specific one: a 'point in dispute' in the sense that there is more than one way of solving a problem. Issue analysis is the method of trying to determine the best way of achieving the general objectives and specific goals set out in the programme statement, having regard to their likely costs and effectiveness.

It is a continuous activity from start to finish of a PPBS exercise, and in education, where the issues raised are formidable in range, numbers and complexity, it is a more vital point of the process than it would be in a service dealing largely with tangibles. There are no right and wrong ways of analysing issues, particularly in education, and if a somewhat narrow procedure appears to be suggested here it is largely in order to put across once again the notion that a systematic approach is vital. It is true that there are vague, apparently unanalysable, nuances in education, but for that very reason it is even more important to try to order as much of this intractable material as possible. But these are merely suggestions, briefly sketched, from which the individual can build his own more elaborate and incisive pattern.

Basically, the approach suggested here is similar to that used in compiling programme statements. Thus the first stage is the drawing up of a scheme designed to show how specific aspects of the whole relate to its particular parts. In the programme statement this is the programme structure: in issue analysis it is the process of establishing the framework, of putting the issue in perspective. Then the objectives relating to a particular part of the statement (or here a particular issue) are defined. Next, measures of need, of provision and performance are applied: this in terms of issue analysis leads to the consideration and evaluation of alternative means of achieving the objective. Costs and effectiveness are set out systematically, and a choice is made. Thereafter the result is fed into the programme planning exercise and given its appropriate priority.

An ordered process

Indeed the procedure is an extension of that used in drawing up the programme statements. The issues themselves will be raised—probably in their hundreds—by the production of the statements, ranging in scope from such far-reaching questions as whether to reorganise secondary education on comprehensive lines, to narrower but still difficult matters like what fees to charge in evening institutes. And the first, highly important, stage in issue analysis, *defining the problem*, can be very much helped by the extent to which the programme statement has been satisfactorily done.

Defining the problem

The programme structure shows how the activity from which the issue arises relates to other activities, and the clarity with which it does this puts the issue into perspective. We can see how critical the issue is to the achievement of the programme category's objectives, and this will indicate how much time and how many people can profitably be used on it. Then, from the needs shown by the programme statement (the clientele or field of action to which a certain standard is to be applied), the scope of the issue—affecting a few people or a hundred thousand, costing a little or a lot—may be seen. The impact of present policies as shown by the programme statement will indicate how much is at stake: a low-cost activity with a very high level of effectiveness will have less scope for improvement through analysis than a costly process that is only 50 per cent effective. And the nature of the issue—specific and tangible or vague and philosophical—will suggest the approach most likely to succeed: for example, whether precise criteria can be calculated or whether a consensus of opinion may be required to set standards.

Setting the target

Having defined the problem, the analyst should *set a target* for the exercise. This should be as precise and objective as possible: for example, to provide within five years pre-school education for 10 per cent of the relevant age group, with extra provision in defined areas of special need ranging from 25 per cent to 35 per cent. As steps towards these specific targets he will need to consider existing levels of provision, deficiencies, and the level of output needed to attain the proposed levels. He will also need to take into consideration any constraints on the programme—such as government policy, or plans in other parts of the service that may conflict.

Working out ways of measuring alternatives

We are using the word 'issue' to refer to a problem with alternative methods of solution (for instance, in the example given the choice might be between providing places in nursery schools or in classes attached to primary schools). So we need a systematic approach to *evaluating the alternatives*. All kinds of criteria can be devised but three main ones are suggested here: costs, effectiveness and practicability.

Isolating *costs* may require ingenuity: both direct and indirect expenses need to be included to give a true picture, for example transport as well as staffing; capital, translated into revenue terms; implications for future years; and possible sources of income. (Thus it would be possible to consider levying charges in order to provide a better standard of service).

Effectiveness is usually difficult, and may be all but impossible, to measure. It may relate to numbers benefited, or to advancing a particular policy, or indeed to a whole range of things, and the kind of measurement possible will depend on the kind of effectiveness we mean and, in turn, on whether we are dealing with quantitative matters or values. Amongst the measures we can try are: direct; e.g. how many school places or teachers have been provided; indirect; for example, not how many good citizens have we turned out but how many fewer children have been in trouble; or parallel; for example, not how much prolonged avoidable absence from school has been prevented, but how quickly the education welfare service can identify and respond to possible causes of trouble. Often, however, the only available measure will be the judgment of those best likely to know. This, provided it is organised and not mere hunch, is not to be despised as an indicator of whether a measure is, or is likely to be, effective in achieving an objective.

The interrelating of these criteria as cost–effectiveness analysis has already been mentioned in chapter 4. In this context it is a way of focusing on the overall aim of securing best value for money across a range of services by relating the measure of effectiveness to a unit of cost: to have a ten-minute reaction time by an education welfare officer to a reported problem may be possible but, when costed, not worth the money compared with other possible benefits. Testing the value for money of a project may relate to achieving a particular standard for the lowest possible cost, or alternatively to achieving the best possible results for a given cost.

Practicability covers a range of measures that, whatever the logic of analysis, may have to be taken into account. Constraints must be. For example, it is no use proving that nursery education for underprivileged children is a cheaper and better approach than comprehensive schools for all if government policy prevents the one and encourages the other. (On the other hand the possibility of getting national policies changed as a result of systematic analysis of costs and effectiveness should not be discounted. When assumption so often takes the place of facts or research in framing policy, a really trenchant study of realities at local level can be influential. It can also challenge the natural tendency to standardise without regard to local needs.)

For practical purposes, though, these constraints have to be accepted. So, too, do those of time, availability of materials, public opinion and so on. A wonderfully cost–effective project that cannot be mounted or completed before a strict deadline—say the date for raising the school-leaving age—may be useful as a training exercise but will achieve little else. Nor can exercises be accepted as valid if they fail to take into account, for instance, whether there is space available to build new kitchens and dining rooms at the schools where they are most needed.

And, perhaps most important of all, the aspiring analyst will usually have to bear in mind that, however logical, his conclusions will need to satisfy a lot of people if they are to become reality. The general public and the teaching profession are two important groups whose attitudes may be formed by other criteria than those of the analyst. Whether he takes into account possible political attitudes will depend perhaps as much on the administrator's courage as on his judgment: at any rate he will be wise to bear in mind that they exist. A checklist of clearances needed for any scheme and a plan of campaign in the event of failure may save him endless trouble.

Thinking up alternative approaches

At this point analysis temporarily may become less important than imagination. Having defined the problem and weighed up costs and benefits, we need radical thinking to be sure that all the possible kinds of action have been considered. This is where an operational research approach may be of most value, bringing all types of mind and background experience to bear, making sure as far as possible that the outcome is not restricted by the failure of an individual to climb out of his personal rut—one can have too much expertise and experience. The techniques of think-tanks and brain-storming sessions are well enough known by now to need no elaboration here. It is important though, to be sure that hierarchies and conventions do not deprive the exercise of useful ideas. The analysis comes later: at this point a stream-of-consciousness technique recording ideas, questions and possibilities is likely to serve the purpose best.

The alternatives that are being sought can be applied to both costs and effectiveness (if we assume that we can do little about practicability). On costs the possibilities are normally restricted to two general approaches—either reducing expenditure or increasing income—but these can be sufficient provided that the need to question assumptions and to take nothing for granted is accepted. So far as effectiveness is concerned the potential range is limitless though much more radical thinking may be needed. New trends of thought, new systems, new techniques, up-to-date research—any of these may supply a clue. Efficiency exercises may help and so may simplifying procedures (here the scraping-to-the-bone effect of the programme statement analysis may show its value in focusing on essentials).

Assessing the merits of the various possibilities

The next stage may also show the benefit of a team approach to issue analysis, or at least of subjecting the process to outside scrutiny, since it is hard to look entirely objectively at alternatives if one of them includes the way one has done it oneself for years.

The first move is to try to calculate the probable performance of each possibility according to the chosen criteria. This may need no more than simple arithmetic, or it may be susceptible to prediction by mathematical formulae or reducible to manageable terms by using a computer: in education, on the other hand, where cause and effect are not so easy to predict, it will be necessary to indicate the assumptions on which the calculation is made and to place correspondingly less reliance on them when the next step is attempted. This is the evaluation itself, and is simply the comparison of the possibilities as illustrated by the previous calculation. Again, education usually makes this less precise than might be desirable, and the process tends to resolve itself into a matter of 'on the one hand this, on the other hand that', a comparison usually known as a *trade-off*.

The most likely trade-off in cost–effectiveness analysis is *cost against effectiveness*: it may cost less to send pre-school children part-time to nursery classes, but will this be as effective as sending them full-time? A similar contradistinction may be *quality against quantity*: if you admit more children to nursery school can you give the necessary attention to each child? One trade-off may spark off another (*effectiveness* 1 *against effectiveness* 2) for it can be argued that half a day properly used is much more effective for young children than a whole day, which would be too tiring for them to keep up the pace. *Effectiveness (or cost) against practicability* will often arise, of course. *Short-term against long-term* effectiveness, or costs, may give very different results. Finally, *certainty against risk* may be the choice. This of course is the classical dilemma of the businessman who may see a splendid way to increase his profits but not without venturing what he already has. (Most people, it seems, either intuitively or by mathematics, follow a course known as mini-max, the maximum profit from the least risky approach. Educationists are not usually in the position of taking great risks so the equation may be simpler for them.)

Choosing a course of action

Having chosen what seems the best course it is important to test each link in the chain of argument, to see what assumptions have been made and how much a wrong assumption can affect the outcome. The process is that of measuring the sensitivity of each part: that is,

Table 16   Pre-school education: possible ways of spending £200,000 annually

Possibility	Annual cost per place (£)	Numbers of children	Effectiveness Educational potential (A)	(B)	Convenience to parents
Nursery schools 1 Full-time attendance	200	1,000	Separate unit in charge of nursery school head	Theoretically 100% but is this too long a day?	100%
2 Part-time attendance	100	2,000	Separate unit in charge of nursery school head	Theoretically 50% but this may be long enough day	Less useful to many, particularly those who work
Nursery classes 3 Full-time attendance	100	2,000	Under control of infant school head	As in 1 above	100%
4 Part-time attendance	50	4,000	Under control of infant school head	As in 2 above	As in 2 above
5 Mixture 10% of 1 above 20% of 2 above 20% of 3 above 50% of 4 above	85 average	3,000 approx.	As in 1—4 above	As in 1—4 above	As in 1—4 above

looking systematically at each stage to see how an alteration affects the next stage and so on. If a quantity can be given to each variable, such as a percentage, so much the better. Then the process is to repeat the calculations assuming (i) the best and (ii) the worst. These variations, of course, may affect the degree of risk or other trade-offs and thus may lead to a revised choice.

Analysing issues 135

Issues for analysis

(i) Clearly the analysis and its accompanying paperwork can be very elaborate. It would be outside the scope of this brief introduction to the process to demonstrate techniques in detail: to a large extent they have, in any event, to be devised by the analyst to meet his own

		Practicability		Notes
Ages	Sites	Public opinion	Teacher opinion	
2—4+	None in districts 3, 4 and 6	Favourable	Generally favourable as this is existing assumption	In many ways desirable, but a luxury, and open to objection as to length of day
2—4+	As in 1 above	Less favourable generally, but twice as many mothers would qualify	Reluctance to deal with two sets of pupils daily	Reduced costs and removes objection in 1 above
3—4+	No problem	As for 1 above	Resistance from nursery school teachers?	Same costs as in 2 above, but although in many ways desirable open to objection on length of day and possible resistance by teachers
3—4+	As in 3 above	As for 2 above	Probably least acceptable	Most children covered but several objections
As in 1—4 above	Removes problem at 1	Should be favourable	Would enable existing schools to remain	Recommended as attempt to resolve difficulties and yet increase provision

particular needs. A simple example is given in Table 16. Needless to say, this is but a part, considerably over-simplified, of what an analysis of such a complex problem might be like; needless to say, too, the figures and the comments are purely illustrative.

(ii) Having looked at this, and perhaps quickly detected its many deficiencies, the reader may like to try his hand. The following notes might, for instance, provide the raw material for analysing possible ways of organising adult education classes.

Adult education in Dullton: direct provision by LEA

Target: to reach standard of enrolment without increasing net cost to the authority

Clientele: adult population, 200,000

Standards: 5% to enrol for classes

Provision: 3% enrol   (National average 4%)

	1	2	3	4	5
Attendance by District:	6%	1%	4%	2%	2%
Distribution of centres: (all of equal sizes)	5	2	8	1	6
Average distribution: (miles between centres)	$\frac{1}{2}$	4	$\frac{3}{4}$	2	$\frac{1}{4}$
Social needs indicators of districts: (high is greatest need)	0·4	0·9	0·5	0·7	0·5

Total annual expenditure: £46,000

Income from fees: £6,000

Annual enrolment fee per student: £2 for all courses

Lecturers' fees: £2·50 for two-hour class

No. of lecturers: 300

Average no. per class: 10   No. of classes: 300

Length of courses: 36 weeks

Possibilities and relevant factors:
How many centres? Where? How big?
How high fees? Differential fees—according to subject or income (? admin. costs)
For whom intended? Easy payment fees? Sales resistance?
Publicity: costs? effectiveness?
Close centres? Close classes? On what basis? Reduce length of course?

   Relevance of traditional evening institutes to (a) modern and (b) working-class interests.

14 The system applied

Throughout the book I have tried to emphasise that PPBS and its characteristic process of issue analysis are not finite, self-contained methods of obtaining precise answers to all the fundamental planning problems in the social services. Rather, they fulfil two main functions. The first is to apply a systematic analysis to creative and ancillary activities, and by so doing to challenge assumptions and provide if possible a surer basis for value judgments. The second, and contrasting, function is to explore the implications of this analysis by following promising directions of investigation into possible new ground. So there is never an end point nor a completely finished exercise. Once the exploration of new ground has been completed the new territory is incorporated into the central analytical process; this has the effect of creating consequential further issues for analysis; and so the process goes on. For those who seek instant solutions to management questions this is less than satisfactory: for those who accept that in management there are no absolute solutions, and certainly no quick ones, it offers a stimulating yet ordered method as a basis for planning.

To implement a complete planning system based on these methods would, for an education authority or a university or large college, take several years, quite a lot of manpower and the agreement of those holding the purse-strings. Even where it is decided to introduce the system there is likely to be a transitional period in which the new method overlaps with the old; during this time PPBS is in effect being used as a means of sharpening administrative perceptions and looking at educational problems from new angles. In this it can have a most salutary effect.

This aspect of the system can be applied at any level, by an individual as well as an authority, a school as well as a ministry. It is here, therefore, that radical changes in the style of planning—through emphasis on educational rather than organisational or technical questions, and, along with this, greater participation by educators— can most easily be initiated. Consequently this final chapter begins with practical illustrations of how a start can be made.

Beginnings

To set down all the activities of even a relatively small institution, such as a primary school, would be a formidable task, one perhaps sufficiently daunting to inhibit the launching of a new approach. To do so for an education authority could be a full-time job in itself. The prospect of analysing all these activities and then plotting their inter-relationships stretches the imagination to breaking point. The initial task should be something more modest. If we accept a time-span of several years for the adoption of a full-scale system we can use the first time round to get used to the method; and we shall do very well if we can focus attention while we are doing so on some of the key issues that may need to be analysed, at least in part, before a PPBS exercise can even meaningfully begin.

The next few pages set out the results of a preliminary survey on these lines that might be undertaken by an interested group in an education authority. It is subdivided into eight parts (corresponding to the programme categories used earlier in the book) each one of which might be the subject of study by an individual or smaller group.

Pre-school education

Although provision of pre-school education is a duty of LEAs, the extent and nature of the provision has been limited. The survey begins therefore with a consideration of the proper status of this category within the authority's total programme. Is it a desirable, but unimportant, luxury, or an essential: and if essential, for whom? Is it a 'consumer good' or a basic need?

Hard evidence is, surprisingly, not easy to come by, but research and opinion tends to support the intuitive view of the analyst that pre-school education is a valuable experience particularly for the socially disadvantaged. On the understanding that much more stringent argument and research will be needed the programme statement looks at the level, costs, and effectiveness of present provision, assesses it and considers how best to deploy resources over the succeeding five years. Provision levels are stated in relation to existing constraints: places in nursery schools and percentage of clientele served; places in nursery classes and percentage of clientele served. The desired standard is set down in relation to twenty defined areas of social need and the provision is compared with this, showing only 30 per cent in the eight worst areas and no coherent pattern within these eight. Staffing and other costs are worked out and show that nursery schools, which have their own heads and are in separate premises, cost much more than nursery classes, but that they take pupils from the age of two to four-plus compared with three to four-plus in nursery classes.

The issue analysis focuses on: whether to have schools or classes; whether to have full-time or part-time places; and how to improve provision in areas of social need. Action programmes are devised to implement the recommendations.

Issues for future analysis include: the relationship of statutory to voluntary agencies, such as those providing private nurseries and pre-school playgroups; and links with day nurseries run by social services departments.

Primary education

The programme statement seeks to measure the authority's performance against the principles and standards of the Plowden Report, particularly (i) the educational priority area concept as it affects numbers, deployment and quality of staff and standards of premises; and (ii) the organisation of the service, including size of schools and ages and stages of transfer.

The authority's present and projected school population is considered in relation to available school places, first overall, then according to likely population movement within the area, and third according to the twenty areas of social need. Accommodation is looked at with a view to possible restrictions in class size, having regard to the space available, and zoning schemes are considered. Quality is then considered according to specified criteria. The pattern emerges of a theoretical surplus of largely sub-standard building in older areas and overcrowded if newer schools on housing estates. The relationship between county and voluntary schools, some of which are considerably overcrowded, is considered.

Plowden's criteria of size are applied and many of the sub-standard buildings prove also too small. Possible closures are considered together with repercussions for staffing and new building requirements, the likely effect on public opinion and so on.

Teacher supply is then looked at, first as the schools are at present, and then as they might be if the new standards of size were applied. An overall target figure is suggested and a graduated scale of teacher–pupil ratios is fixed according to social need. Issues for future analysis include: (i) a more radical appraisal of schools in relation to the possibility of first schools and middle schools with transfer to secondary schools at either twelve or thirteen (this has to be examined together with possibilities arising from the secondary education programme), and (ii) measures of educational standards.

Secondary education

Here the programme statement first considers the implications of raising the school-leaving age. The likely increase in school population is worked out and accommodation is assessed, first for quantity, then for quality. Needs here seem less urgent than in the primary schools. Staffing targets are set and related to those in the primary programme.

The small size of many schools seems to limit effective deployment of resources. This also has a bearing on the size of sixth forms, many of which are below the desirable minimum of 120 pupils. More serious, the total number of sixth-formers is well below and compares unfavourably with other authorities.

Size is looked at in relation to re-organisation generally: minor modifications are suggested but the basic question, selective or non-selective, needs further analysis. A joint exercise is initiated with the primary education branch.

It seems likely, however, that there are other deeper causes of the small sixth forms; particularly since fewer stay on after the statutory leaving age than the national and regional average, results in GCE examinations are worse, and fewer go on to higher education. A research programme is designed to investigate this.

Other matters for further analysis are (i) the effect of curriculum and timetabling on the use of resources, and (ii) the amount of discretion to heads of schools to allocate the resources allowed them.

Children with special needs

The programme statement starts from the proposition that it is crucially important to identify as early and as accurately as possible children with various handicaps if they are to be given help at a time when it can do most good.

So far as learning problems are concerned, existing provision has leant heavily on special schools for the educationally subnormal: there are more places than the national average. The significance and implications of this are considered. Further analysis suggests that some 60 per cent of children admitted to these schools are not 'innately' ESN but that they are severely socially handicapped. As 65 per cent are of secondary school age it seems that problems are not being identified early enough. Again, the numbers in special schools with genuinely low IQS appear to be smaller than they should be according to the standard distribution curve, so some problems appear to go undetected. Identification is suggested as a first priority and specific standards are laid down.

A similar exercise is carried out for children with emotional and behavioural, with physical, and with severe social handicap; and staffing needs are worked out having regard to the interrelationship of the various handicaps. The areas of highest incidence are assessed, using the twenty areas of social need as a basis, and co-operating teams of doctors, psychologists, social workers and education welfare officers are recommended, weighting the numbers of staff appropriately. An ordered system of screening and referral from the schools is proposed.

Then treatment is considered: first, the effectiveness of existing provision, and then the changes required to take account of new patterns of identification. Peripatetic remedial services and units attached to ordinary schools are proposed, replacing much separate school provision. However, some former schools for the educationally subnormal can be adapted for use by maladjusted children, for whom a growing need is demonstrated. Careful attention is given to locating new schools according to the area analysis and changes in age ranges are proposed.

A programme of gradual change is devised, to allow for the gradual effects of new policies and new methods of identification and care is taken to see that the programme can be adjusted in case the effects are not exactly as predicted.

Several hundred further issues remain to be analysed.

School meals

The programme statement compares the numbers taking school meals with the national average and finds a substantial short-fall, although the numbers qualifying for free meals is above average. The question is looked at in relation to the twenty areas of social need, where there is a variation from 80 per cent meals (with only 5 per cent free) in one area to 45 per cent (with 25 per cent free) in another. These variations are studied in relation to dining arrangements and some correlation is found between good facilities and meals taken; yet economics seems a major factor. However, in certain areas where convenience foods are used instead of conventionally cooked meals consumption is higher even where there is economic need.

A revised programme of new dining facilities is proposed, in conjunction with the primary and secondary education programmes. New financial arrangements are proposed including part-payments by families who just fail to qualify for free meals.

Further analysis is directed towards the possibility of replacing all traditional meals by frozen and other convenience foods.

Recreational, social and cultural education

This programme statement looks at youth service, community work and adult education. The basic difference between this and earlier programme categories is that participation is voluntary (this and its recreational tradition implies that fees can be charged), so that much thought has to be given to objectives and appropriate levels of provision.

Youth service is considered first, by age. Of the under-fourteens some 24 per cent belong to an organisation of some kind, about half to voluntary uniformed groups, and a third to the authority's recreation clubs held in schools. Of the over-fourteens a slightly lower proportion take part, and there is a dramatic fall-off after the age of fifteen for girls and sixteen for boys. Voluntary church groups have the highest membership, the authority's own provision is less than for the under-fourteens and the specialist voluntary youth organisations make some provision. An enquiry is launched into the reasons for this pattern of provision and the needs of the future having regard to the interests of young people.

Next the situation is considered in the twenty areas of social need. There is some evidence of heavier provision of clubs in areas of greatest need but attendance at many of these clubs is low, suggesting a lack of attractive power. The quality of buildings is considered and those in the suburbs are generally of higher standard. Commercial facilities are well patronised.

Thirdly, the relative costs of the activities both to the authority and in total are looked at. It seems that the voluntary church groups are least costly to the LEA, and the voluntary youth organisations by far the most costly, particularly on the basis of cost per enrolled member.

The issues analysed are: (i) whether traditional club and recreational provision should continue to be emphasised or whether counselling and guidance is now more needed; (ii) whether leadership particularly of the informal kind should now be given highest priority; and (iii) what training programmes are needed. Policies regarding the use of school premises are reviewed, bearing in mind both the possible new emphasis on counselling and the heavy cost of separate premises.

A further study is initiated into the relative needs for general and specialist recreation facilities.

Organised community centres cater for only 2 per cent of the population, and future policy is considered in relation to areas of need, costs and new patterns of living. The question of separate or combined youth and community services is analysed. Community organisation and community development are seen as great and growing needs, and the statement poses the question of whether this need can be met by the authority's own staff or specially appointed new ones, or whether assistance to voluntary bodies is more appropriate.

Relationships with voluntary bodies are considered generally with regard to costs, public attitudes to authority, and possible narrow objectives of voluntary bodies. Action research projects are instituted.

In adult education direct provision (mainly in evening centres) and assistance to university extra-mural and WEA programmes are considered. Use made of evening centres is less than the national average, conspicuously so in certain of the twenty areas. The relevance of traditional evening centres to the various sectors of society is considered, and contemporary popular cultural trends are listed and compared with actual provision. Costs, fees and fee collection, recruitment programmes, advertising and the location of centres are all considered and a revised programme is produced. Staffing needs and organisation are reviewed and full-time organisers and teacher-training programmes are recommended. Policy in relation to grant-aiding WEA and university classes is considered, bearing in mind the lower class fees and higher tuition fees of these bodies.

Future analysis, taking into account the findings of the Russell Committee on Adult Education, is to be directed towards the scope, orientation and organisation of adult education, including library and physical recreation services.

Youth employment

The programme statement begins by analysing the arguments for and against the authority's continuing to operate the service, in the context of national deliberations about whether its future properly lies as a branch of education or of the Department of Employment. Consideration of its declared objectives strengthens the argument for the present arrangements.

Quantitative aspects are considered in relation to secondary school reorganisation; the needs of a raising of the school-leaving age; the likely economic situation, and possible changes in the range of responsibility of the service as a result of national legislation. The criteria of the Central Youth Employment Executive are applied to staffing, taking into account local circumstances, and effectiveness is measured by looking at the amount of information and advice given, the public response to the service, and the use made of it by employers.

A special study is made, in relation to the children with special needs programme statement, of the requirements of handicapped young people, including the unsettled and recent immigrants. Deployment of resources is looked at in the light of the twenty areas of social need, and reorganisation is proposed to match the proposed creation of five area teams under the children with special needs programme.

Further analysis is to include co-operation with schools and colleges and the relationship of the service with their careers and guidance programmes.

Further education

The last programme category, further education, appears to need a different approach from the others. As with recreational, social and cultural education, participation is essentially voluntary and there is difficulty in assessing appropriate levels of provision. Fees can be charged (though they are often met from grants paid by this or other authorities), and courses provided in one authority attract substantial out-county payments from other authorities whose students may attend the home authority's colleges. Furthermore, the costs of advanced further education and teacher training are met from national pools, to which authorities contribute regardless of the level of provision they themselves may make.

The programme statement concerns itself largely therefore with new ways of looking at the budget and the management of further education institutions. Its general slant is towards obtaining value for money rather than towards limiting expenditure, particularly for advanced work. It looks first at promoting the further education of the authority's students, whether locally or further afield, and second at local provision, whether for local students or those from further afield.

As far as promoting the education of local students is concerned, the pooling of costs means that whether value for money is obtained depends on the proportion of local students who take advanced courses, regardless of where they are held. In fact, as the secondary education programme showed, the proportion going on to higher education is below the national average, so the pool contribution per student is higher than the average. Investigation of the causes of this is therefore highly important and it seems likely that better value for money in further education may depend largely on efforts in the early stages of the service and on social factors generally.

The implication for the second element, direct provision of courses, is that, since the direct costs are reimbursed from the pool, advanced courses should, theoretically, be expanded, thus removing one of the possible causes for low attendance, i.e. the need to leave home. However, there are constraints on how many advanced courses can be provided locally, such as the decisions of the Regional Advisory Council. In any event, education authorities are not in competition, like businesses, and there is an obligation for them to co-operate in rationalising provision and to promote, in the national interest, efficiency and economy in the colleges they maintain.

Performance measures are therefore suggested to enable colleges to compare themselves with each other and with national standards, particularly with regard to (i) the use made of the plant, (ii) staff–student ratios, (iii) size of classes, (iv) proportions of successful students and (v) costs per student. A pattern is outlined in which student demand and productivity are used to plan future courses and decide whether existing ones should continue or not. In order to encourage this review and possible pruning, maximum freedom is recommended for colleges to allocate their resources, within given estimates, to best advantage: any savings, for example, from increased efficiency, should operate to the advantage of those making the savings.

A particular issue relating to fees is deferred for further analysis. On the one hand it seems desirable to encourage differential fees so that different colleges or different departments of particular colleges might increase their income. On the other hand general public policy has to be considered: should students in engineering pay higher fees than those in the social sciences, simply because the latter cost less since they need less expensive equipment and may manage with larger classes? Furthermore, courses earning high income are not necessarily those most needed in relation to vocational opportunities.

Although these principles are more directly relevant to advanced courses and teacher training, they can perhaps solve a serious problem if they are also applied to colleges doing lower-level work. The effect of the different methods of financing advanced and other work in colleges run by the same authority is often unfortunate. There is less incentive to authorities to prune the estimates of polytechnics since to do so has little effect on rate-borne expenditure: therefore cuts imposed in further education tend to fall on the other institutions, sometimes with dire results, and particularly on those needing a lot of equipment or materials. It seems desirable, therefore, to apply the same criteria, suitably modified to take account of the level of work: that is, not to seek to impose an overall limit of expenditure but to introduce incentives to high productivity and evaluation of performance. In any event, it should be possible to allow credit for fee income and income from out-county payments when considering the actual costs to the authority.

Incentives and organisation

Although the question of incentives is raised in its most piquant form in considering the further education programme category, it must inevitably run like a thread throughout any survey of issues in educational planning and budgeting. It is the point at which the matter of participation by practitioners in the planning exercise is put to the test.

It is also a practical complement to the theoretical arguments advanced earlier in this book for a new style of planning based on the closely related philosophical needs of the planning and educating processes. The complexities of educational provision are such, the argument goes, that at many points external control is impractical, in which case the prudent course is to build into the process strong inducements for the practitioner to scrutinise his own activities. Sometimes it may be enough simply to give the practitioner the opportunity to do so: for example, to allow the head of a school to decide how his final allocation of budget resources is to be made even though he played no part in building up the estimate; or better still, to invite him to indicate priorities when submitting his proposals. Still better results may come from adding incentives.

We have reached the point, in fact, at which we should consider the implications of the approach for organisation (reversing, be it noted, the usual process in which the organisation is settled first and then, with luck, a thought is spared for the implications of the organisation for methods of working). After a thorough and thoroughly successful PPBS exercise, I have suggested, the appropriate organisation to carry out the approved plan should be immediately apparent. It will be different for different tasks and different institutions, so too-ambitious generalisations would be of little value, even if we had completed a full-scale exercise. Even the limited analysis attempted here, however, suggests two general points that might be borne in mind, both stemming from consideration of incentives.

The first relates to actual financial incentives. Too often schools, colleges and education committees are expected, apparently, to devote time and ingenuity to ways of saving money without any pay-off for themselves. I am not suggesting, of course, five new pence to the administrator for every pound saved, but some way in which his service, and more particularly his own corner of it, may gain from his efforts. If a general edict goes out that, for instance, further education fees are to go up by 25 per cent, the reaction of college principals is predictable if the money gained is poured into the desert sands of the treasurer's department. It is no use to explain to him that the courses he provides cost infinitely more than even the new fee—no use, that is, in planning terms. He may understand and accept the need for the increase, but he would be able to put this understanding to more practical effect if he knew that the increased revenue would go directly towards improving further education facilities, preferably in his own institution. He himself would be in an infinitely stronger position in relation to his own heads of department if he could offer the same incentives to them. What hope is there that Bloggs will cheerfully accept, still less propose, increasing his class sizes or his staff's hours of work, if he knows that Buggins and not he stands to gain most from the deal?

(In arguing thus I do not, let me add, deny that altruism and public spirit exist, nor even that they exist on a substantial scale. It is simply that I would not personally rely heavily on it as a motive force in producing realistic estimates or staffing forecasts. Further, it does not seem to me proper to do so, for if—as they usually are—Bloggs and Buggins are enthusiasts for their subjects or the work of their departments, then it is less than just arbitrarily to divert the fruits of their enthusiasm to the benefit of other people's subjects or departments.)

The second point extends the argument from this basis to the question of general incentives through discretion, trust and freedom for members of an institution. One of the implications of PPBS is that, once resources have been allocated for the purpose of reaching agreed programme objectives, then there can and should be maximum delegation to those operating the programmes. They should have freedom to adjust their tactics in the light of experience. It could be argued that the orientation of PPBS is towards centralised decision-making on priorities and that this calls for a centralised and hierarchical administrative machine. Yet the aim is not merely centralised decision-making, but decision-making from which many of the arbitrary elements have been removed. Standards and performance measures are declared, laid on the table for all to see, and, as far as possible, applied equally to all. In contrast, nothing is more arbitrary than an *ex officio* pronouncement by a hierarchical superior.

PPBS accepts that there have to be decisions on priorities but it makes ground rules for those who make the decisions as well as for those who make a case for resources for their own particular activities. It provides a framework for testing assumptions and strengthening value judgments. In education, where value judgments must inevitably play a bigger part than in most services, it is doubly important that these ground rules are understood and observed by everyone.

Conclusion

This book ends, as it began, by emphasising that it makes no claim to offer wand-waving solutions to the profound problems that beset educational planning. Indeed from the introduction onwards I have pointed out that its concern is less with providing ready-made answers than with seeing that relevant questions are asked. This is characteristic, too, of the particular planning system it describes. The aim has

been to indicate possible starting-points rather than inevitable conclusions.

This is not to suggest that I have adopted a neutral stance on all,
or even on any, of the matters that have been discussed. Anyone who
argues for a transformation in educational planning is likely to have
strong convictions on the subject. The hope is that, since one of these
convictions is that there are no absolute and final answers in human
affairs, the worst excesses of dogmatism may be avoided. There is a
difference between a conviction and an article of faith. Thus, although
the book argues strongly for participation in educational planning,
this is urged, not simply as a democratic right, still less as a sentimen-
tal panacea based on involvement as a royal road to crisp and effective decision-making, but rather as a way out of a dilemma.

The aim of this participation should not, I have suggested, be to
seek adjustments in the distribution of organisational power, for
this seems easier to relate to the balancing acts we perform to ensure
steady state than to the exploratory thrusts of planning for the future.
Nor should it focus attention on techniques, which are means not
ends. Its basis should rather be a reorientation arising from the perception of fundamental similarities between the needs in educating
and in planning.

These needs centre on understanding as a prelude to controlling
with communication as an integral factor. The systems approach
seems to offer a suitable philosophical framework and a valuable
technique of analysis as a basis for a common language by which
those working in the education service can take new planning initiatives. In particular, a systems approach, which is in any event
needed as a unifying discipline in teaching, can by relating the teaching and the planning processes enable teachers to play a key part in
planning.

From systems thinking as an underlying concept this book has
indicated various implications for administrative methods based on
a movement away from governmental or institutional management
styles of thought towards analytical techniques. In particular it has
considered the contribution that could be made by a planning—programming—budgeting system as a means of linking the essential
management processes of drawing up programmes and allocating
resources. PPBS exemplifies the systems approach and is capable of
being developed as a total system. Here, however, it has appeared
in a more modest guise, as a means of stimulating thought.

No doubt this book has given ample evidence of the difficulties of
applying PPBS to education. I hope nevertheless that it may also have
given some small indication of its potential, for I believe that it
could be the means—whether fully implemented or simply forming
the basis of an approach to analysing important issues—of transform-

ing educational planning. Educational planning certainly needs to be transformed if the service is to stand any chance of meeting the challenges of the twin, and generally conflicting, demands of efficiency and democracy.

Index